Ethical Confrontation in Counseling

John C. Hoffman

Ethical Confrontation in Counseling

CEDAR CREST COLLEGE LIBRARY
ALLENTOWN, PA. 18104

The University of Chicago Press
Chicago and London

792970

The University of Chicago Press, Chicago 60637
The University of Chicago Press, Ltd., London

© 1979 by The University of Chicago
All rights reserved. Published 1979
Printed in the United States of America
83 82 81 80 79   54321

Library of Congress Cataloging in Publication Data

Hoffman, John Charles, 1931–
  Ethical confrontation in counseling.

  Includes bibliographical references and index.
  1. Pastoral counseling. 2. Ethics. 3. Psychotherapy. I. Title. [DNLM: 1. Counseling. 2. Ethics.
3. Morals. 4. Psychotherapy. WM420.3 H699e]
BV4012.2.H55   253.5   78–11799
ISBN 0–226–34785–0

JOHN C. HOFFMAN, an ordained minister in the United Church
of Canada, is professor of religious studies and principal of Iona
College at the University of Windsor.

To Nettie for many reasons

Contents

Preface

This work represents the convergence of two concerns which have long been part of my thinking. Because of a personal career that includes graduate education and teaching experience in organic chemistry, psychotherapy, and theology, my desire to bring such disparate fields of study into a more fruitful engagement has inevitably become part of a search for personal wholeness, or at least for a fuller reconciliation of vocational roles. The present study endeavors quite specifically to engage two of these, theology and psychotherapy—more accurately, theologians and psychotherapists—in a meaningful discussion. Each group can gain useful insights from such encounters and can glean from the other's experiences. It is my conviction, and one operative in this work, that we must oppose the tendency to divide up problems, assigning them to the special responsibility of one discipline or another. The most urgent human problems do not lend themselves to such narrow disciplinary solutions.

One such issue is the nature of the healing process. At least since Freud's time we have increasingly recognized the transforming impact of unconditional acceptance, of being liberated from the need to earn the right to be through fulfilling an ethical code. Yet at some point, especially for those engaged in pastoral care but ultimately, too, for most therapists, healing also becomes a matter of moral decisions, and one senses an uneasiness with all scrupulous attempts to avoid ethical confrontation in therapy. It has long been my conviction that such avoidance is not only morally but also therapeutically wrong and that, furthermore, confrontation need not prevent the simultaneous experience of acceptance. I shall be seeking to argue this case by an appeal to theology and psychotherapeutic theory and experience. This book is not intended as a manual of techniques or even as a series of examples illustrating successful and unsuccessful styles of confrontation. Nor is it an ethical treatise; it does not attempt to validate any particular moral system. Rather, it simply argues that the very nature of the healing process, seen from the perspective of the psychotherapist as well as the theologian, examined in terms of mental health as well as salvation, demands both acceptance and ethical confrontation. Moreover, tapping creative minds in both fields, it presents the claim that a union of acceptance and challenge is actually possible. Not that it is easy. Often we may fail, but if we are unaware that the goal is attainable, we shall not even attempt it. I leave to another time or another writer further explication of this union as a matter of technique. My first desire is to oppose the assumption of so many that it is an impossible task.

As with any work that represents a theme to which one has returned many times over the years, there are numerous people who have guided and encouraged my reflections, including some colleagues who have stubbornly declared it an impossible dream. I would especially acknowledge four who helped to set me upon what I have come to believe is the right track. Roger Shinn and Daniel Day Williams of Union Theological Seminary encouraged my ethical assault on the problem, with the latter urging me to continue the work for publication. Dr. Gotthard Booth taught me much not only about psychotherapy but also about the necessity to raise theological questions concerning the whole enterprise. Finally, my colleague and friend Bob Reeves, chaplain of the Columbia Presbyterian Medical Center in New York City, did much to baptize me into the field of pastoral care. In pursuing this work beyond where I was with them, I hope I have been true to their teaching and their trust. Throughout the whole period I have been supported by my wife, especially at those times when my own academic conscience would deny my right to be "without the book." Finally, I would express my appreciation to Mrs. Geraldine Bryant, who typed not only the final version of this work but also several earlier drafts.

June 1978   Windsor, Ontario

1 "To Heal or Rebuke"
Is That the Question?

A friend of mine who has been deeply involved in the struggles for social justice once remarked that I would be more effective as a theologian were it not for my training in psychotherapy. Such comments reflect an all too prevalent split between psychology and ethics, between mental health and social reform. So one asks, "Is the sexual deviant sick, or is he sinful?" "Is the alcoholic to be pitied or rebuked?" "Is the industrial tycoon insecure or greedy?" Perhaps more to the point, "Is the solution tender, loving care or a good dose of moral indignation?" Too often the issues are understood as if these were the only alternatives. One cannot conduct psychotherapy, it is argued, and also be a moral arbiter; nor can he launch a campaign for social justice against corrupt and selfish men and women if he is going to accept them as they are. It is almost as if society must be divided into those for whom we care and those whom we chastise, as if we must choose to be lovers or moralists.

In theological terms this dilemma reflects the classical tension between law and gospel, between the holiness and the love of God, a tension, to be sure, resolved with varying success in different doctrinal systems. Yet those schooled in such traditions often shift moment by moment between a God of pure accepting love, who in the words of popular sentimentality will always say, "I forgive," and a God who is the righteous Judge whose wrath is revealed against all unrighteousness unto the third and fourth generations. Faced with such a dilemma, many individuals would of course never think of looking to theology for guidance. Let me express our tension in more secular images. The nineteenth century gave the world two apostate Jews of great genius, Karl Marx and Sigmund Freud. In themselves and in the movements they brought into being, they incarnate on one hand social criticism together with moral action and on the other a compassionate drive to understand and to heal. Such is the case whether or not one agrees with the moral and economic analysis of Communist theory or the therapeutic procedures of psychoanalysis. We could then express our tension not as law and gospel, holiness and love, but as Marx and Freud. (It is interesting to note in this context the great influence of the whole psychotherapeutic movement in modern pastoral care and the growing place of Marxist thought in contemporary liberation theologies.)

Must we automatically assume a conflict between the social worker or psychologist and the police officer or judge, with clerics on either side as sentimentalists or puritanical moralists, depending upon temperament or ecclesiastical allegiance? Assuredly, I would not deny that policemen as policemen are more apt to respond immediately in terms of law enforcement, cultural norms, and society's ethic, whereas social workers, especially in a counseling situation, are often professionally oriented toward an understanding attitude which is reluctant to pass judgment. But surely this does not mean that we function best or most humanly in such mutually exclusive roles. I suspect that no thoughtful parent, confronting a wayward child picked up by the police, has ever escaped the awful tension between forgiving love and righteous judgment. He is caught between the desire to embrace that very child who has caused the heartache and a deep sense of moral realities which must not be flouted, between the desire to take that son or daughter into his arms and the need to honor ethical imperatives which must be expressed, no matter how distressing. This is not simply an oddity in the psychological makeup of parents but a reflection of two fundamental truths of the human situation. Without love, acceptance, forgiveness, there is no healing, no regeneration, no restoration of a broken life or a poisoned relationship. But equally, without a strong moral witness which is willing to affirm goodness and condemn evil, without the courage to risk oneself and one's relationships for moral principles, a people perish. The rise of Hitler's Reich witnesses to the latter truth; the continuing estrangement that separates Jew from Palestinian in the Near East, Roman Catholic from Protestant in Ulster, exhibits the former. How can we possibly keep them together?

I propose to address in detail only one side of this tension, to speak to those engaged in therapy or, more accurately, to all of us who are called upon to be therapeutic at times. Therefore I address myself not only to social workers, psychologists, and pastors but also to teachers, parents, and friends, whether or not they are familiar with the special knowledge of psychotherapy or varieties of effectiveness training, to all men and women who seek to understand and heal. (I leave to another time the task of establishing the role of accepting love at the heart of ethical witness, social reform, and moral outrage.) I am appealing for a more consistent and enthusiastic moral witness at the very heart of the psychotherapeutic process, for an end to the assumption that one is exclusively either a healer or a reformer, and for a recognition that true healing (even true psychological healing) must involve a confrontation with the moral realities of life.

Therapy, after all, is conducted in a real world where human beings do not just lie on the analyst's couch, express their feelings openly in the safety of the therapy group, or receive electrical shock treatments. It is a part of a world in which people dream and build, curse and kill, laugh and love, suffer and die. To be mentally whole is to be able to cope with such a world. If you and I would be mentally whole, we cannot deny entire dimensions of reality and live as if there were no question of moral values.

What are the moral realities of our time? Whether or not our age is fundamentally different from any other, it is surely one marked by a series of moral issues of profound human significance. We have killed more people violently in the course of this century than in any other era, and we have yet to use our most efficient weapons. We have witnessed genocide raised to a fine art by one of the most educated, cultured, and humanly productive nations of Europe. We have seen "a war to end all wars" prepare the rich soil for a greater war, only to be followed by a Cold War.

To be sure, our history is not all bleak. We have also experienced the first modern attempts to form an effective world government. As much as one-fifth of the world's population—largely nonwhites—has gained political independence from mainly white colonial rule. In the industrialized West real strides have been made toward greater economic justice. Mass movements for liberation are presently sweeping the globe, filling the air with phrases like "women's liberation," "gay liberation," "black power," "people power" and creating a confrontation between the First and Third Worlds. The underfed, underemployed, ill-housed majority of the earth are no longer content that an overdeveloped minority should consume many times their fair share of the world's resources. They demand a new economic order either through moral reason, debating the issues at United Nations conferences, or through violence. No man, they cry, should further increase his affluence while others are denied the bare essentials of life, food to eat, clean water to drink, a rudimentary sanitation system, a roof over their heads. The nonwhite races demand that their color be seen not as a sign of all that is evil and nonhuman. As Ananias Mpunzi, a black South African, put it, they want the freedom which enables "black people, all black people everywhere, to affirm what they are—*black* people— and ... white people to affirm what they are—just *ordinary* people, even though they are white."[1] Here at home our poor; our black, ethnic, and aboriginal peoples; and our wives, sisters, and daughters are asking for justice which has too often been denied them. Nor should we overlook birth control, euthanasia, homosexuality, abortion, capital punishment—a seemingly unending stream of issues within our personal lives on which key moral decisions must be made.

Yet all of this says nothing of the future. With voices from every religious persuasion, every academic expertise, every political stripe reminding us that the future of the human race and of the world is ours to shape, we can no longer afford merely to wander through history. We must plan a future. We must develop models for a more human and humanizing social and economic structure, all of which means hard moral choices.

This being the world in which you and I would practice therapy, professionally or otherwise, how can we hope to establish a fully creative relationship between the counselee and his world if together we have never faced these issues or acknowledged their existence? I suggest that confronting the ethical imperatives of life is a psychotherapeutic necessity. Moreover, as members of the human race, how could we ignore the larger moral issues for both counselor and counselee? Is it enough if all I do is to lighten the boredom of a suburban housewife or teach a racist how to express his hostility, so that each can continue comfortably perpetuating the exploitation of others? Can we allow intensive group experience to become a psychological substitute for moral transformation, a secular confessional with no repentance? Surely not.

Why the reluctance about ethics in psychotherapy? I think

we can identify at least three factors: (1) a general disillusionment with authority, including moral authorities; (2) the development of covert morality under the guise of psychological (or more broadly scientific) truth, and (3) the problem of moralism.

1. In a sense Watergate has been but the latest and perhaps the most dramatic in a series of disillusionments which have swept the Western world. The unchanging and unchallenged authorities of medieval culture have fallen one by one. The infallible Word of God, the moral rectitude of church and universities, the unquestioned assumption that our way (be it British, American, German, Russian, or even scientific) was *the* way, the sacredness of marriage, the virtue of our heroes—all have been questioned and, for many, found terribly wanting. The day of unshakable authority has ended, never to return. We have been driven from the security of absolute certainty, and, though not always happy with our new surroundings, we cannot make that sort of commitment again. Ethical systems as an infallible moral guide will not sell. Even within the traditionally authoritarian and paternalistic structures of the Roman Catholic church one finds a new appeal to individual conscience where men and women can claim their place as good Catholics while openly opposing the moral teaching of their church on a subject like birth control. Consequently a psychotherapist is in accord with the tenor of the times when he refuses to become the final arbiter in moral issues raised by his client. He refuses not merely to force the client to take responsibility for his own life (which in itself is a valid objective) but also because he does not believe in moral absolutes. "How many ethical certainties of the past do we now reject?" he might ask, and here we would surely agree with the therapist.

Whoever takes the moral dimension of life seriously must realize that all one possesses is personal experience, probably enriched by the ethical traditions of a community. The counselor can only witness to moral truth as he or she has been able to discern it but can never claim an infallible perception of that truth. Nevertheless, I believe one can *witness* to the truth. That we do not possess the truth with absolute certainty does not mean we are left with no insight at all. Such reasoning could merely be the excuse for a moral cop-out. Peter Berger, writing about sexual ethics, says, "This relativization in the understanding of sexual roles does not, of course, free the individual from finding his own way morally. *That* would be another instance of "bad faith," with the objective fact of relativity being taken as an alibi for the subjective necessity of finding single decisive points at which one engages one's whole being."[2] Berger is contending that the risk of moral error does not preclude a moral commitment. Moreover, I suggest that it would be inaccurate to see this purely as a necessary but blind leap of faith, to argue, like Ivan Karamazov, that if God is dead everything is permitted, ending in a moral nihilism. Surely we do not need eternal moral certitudes in fine detail to know that Auschwitz and Treblinka were a monstrous evil or that there was something undeniably good in Martin Luther King and Helder Camara.

A nihilistic rejection of the whole realm of ethics may be in itself a source of psychopathology. In *The Quest for Identity*, Allen Wheelis comments that the "eternal verities have been lost in excess of our ability to get along comfortably without them."[3] While Wheelis does not look to religion to meet this need, his analysis of the crisis remains significant. The contemporary scene is characterized by a lack of moral identity, of values which can claim man's allegiance, with both social and psychological consequences not to be ignored. Indeed Wheelis concedes that his own discipline (psychotherapy) has contributed to the problem by encouraging a neglect of the will and responsibility, too often urging modern man to put his back to the couch rather than his shoulder to the wheel.

2. Alternatively, one may seek to avoid the issue of ethics by simply dropping the terms and covertly bringing moral judgments back under the name of psychology. How can the therapist avoid such judgments? What of a patient who announces that he is planning to kill his wife that night? Naturally there are psychological judgments to be made here. Is this merely bravado, with no substance in fact, something which he is physically and emotionally incapable of doing, a cry for attention? Or is it a serious proposal? What if it is the latter? The therapist's response in that case entails a moral judgment, and not simply a therapeutic one. He could hardly allow the murder, even if it would greatly accelerate the patient's return to health, but if by some bizarre quirk he would, that in itself represents a moral judgment, not

the absence of an ethical issue. What of a patient who contemplates suicide? Surely the response of his therapist has moral as well as psychotherapeutic elements.

Some therapists openly make moral judgments, seeking to justify their ethic by claiming that it represents not an inevitably "subjective" moral code but a scientifically founded and therefore "objective" guide for action. I suppose the most celebrated examples of such thinking are found in the field of sexual ethics or what many still choose to call sexual ethics. How ironical that the modern psychotherapeutic disciplines, to a large extent the intellectual offspring of Sigmund Freud, have developed exponents of such liberalized sexual mores, when one considers how traditional and "hung up" Freud himself was in many ways! (Though he could write about the importance of the sexual education of children, for example, his own were forced "to learn the facts of life through peepholes and street gossip, just like all the other children of his day.")[4] Now, for some therapists at least, the problems of sexual repression are to be overcome by a free and easy acting out. Albert Ellis is of course one of the more famous exponents of this view, a position he has consistently supported for some twenty years. In *Sex without Guilt* he attacks old moral taboos concerning homosexuality, masturbation, premarital sex, adultery, and so on. Premarital sexual activity is clearly advisable, as it brings sexual and psychological release, added sexual competency, and ego enhancement. Moreover, he concludes that "sex is fun; heterosexual relations, in particular, are the very best fun; and more heterosexual relations are still more fun."[5] To be sure, in this same work he admonishes that it is probably not advisable to engage in adulterous adventures, as these almost inevitably strain the marriage relationship, given the "horrible upbringing"[6] our culture has bequeathed us. In his later writings, however, Ellis seems less skeptical about the possibilities of successful extramarital liaisons and has developed more hope for the possibilities of civilized adultery. He supports his position not by moral argument but by an appeal to what is psychologically healthy. Premarital intercourse for those not hampered by a puritan conscience is a natural and healthy outlet for the sexual drives. But a rose is a rose is a rose, and the mere invocation of psychological considerations alone does not define out of existence the moral dimensions of such issues. To say that it is better for a person to be unencumbered by traditional sexual ethics, and to give free expression to the genital drive both in marriage and out of it, than to be a faithful member of a monogamous relationship, though at times afflicted by an unruly instinct, is a moral more than a therapeutic judgment. Indeed Ellis at least tacitly admits this when he condemns traditional social values as resulting from our "horrible upbringing." The whole area becomes even more fraught with import when one considers the issue of the therapist engaging in sexual relationships with patients to "speed their recovery" or the employment of "sexual surrogates" as a variant behavior modification for sexually troubled male patients. To be sure, it has not remained for religionists and philosophers alone to question this stance in psychotherapy, nor have psychotherapists alone among social scientists offered to resolve moral issues by transforming them into objective science.[7] From within the psychotherapeutic field, Allen Wheelis, in both *The Quest for Identity* and a more recent work, *The Moralist*; Karl Menninger, in *Whatever Became of Sin?* and much earlier O. Hobart Mowrer, in *The Crisis in Psychiatry and Religion*, have all questioned the easy dismissal of ethics by therapists and the wider community. Lest we confuse the issue, however, I am not at this point making the case for marital fidelity or premarital chastity. I am not debating ethics but, rather, the claim by some psychotherapists that to espouse free love on the grounds that it eases one's mind is to avoid ethics. They are simply offering an ethic based upon some form of naturalism, entirely ignoring the human capacity to transcend nature and decide how to relate to it. At the moment, for our argument it is more important to note that Ellis is actually offering ethical injunctions under the guise of psychological observations than to decide whether or not those injunctions are morally sound.

3. The third and most significant source of the psychotherapeutic avoidance of ethics is the fear of moralism. As understood in the vast majority of talking therapies, a primary cause of mental illness is the tyranny of conscience. Men and women can be crippled as truly by the fear of sinning as by sin itself. The experiences of psychotherapy have indeed revealed anew the dreadful wrath of the moral law, the living hell for the one who

knows no "right to be" apart from fulfilling his own or society's ethical code and ideals. Such is the nature of the moralism. For many, however, the therapeutic admonition to stop moralizing has become a call to remove all ethical challenges from the healing encounter. But must we assume that all morality is inevitably moralistic? Let us define the moral realm as that dimension of human experience which arises from man's ability so to transcend himself that he is able to judge self, neighbor, and society by whatever he accepts as truly good. Whether or not this morality must develop a moralistic expression then becomes the crucial question. If so, the tension between psychology and ethics, between healers and reformers, is in fact inevitable, and the therapist must recognize the danger in all moral witness. But if not, then the reconciliation between moral challenge and therapeutic acceptance lies in fostering a nonmoralistic morality. Such is the position I seek to establish.

Even assuming that morality were inevitably moralistic, that therapist, as therapist, would be unwise who sought to avoid ethics entirely. Given the nature of our humanness and of our world, there is no way we can avoid the ethical. To try solving the problem of a moralistic conscience by telling the afflicted to give up ethics would be like advising a husband who is plagued with impotence to stop going to bed with his wife, as if to rule sex out of his life. Is it not a reflection upon us that we think the latter more absurd than the former? If morality is inevitably moralistic, then we need to confront the demon head on. This can no more be done by defining it out of existence, by denying the reality of the moral dimension of life, than the impotent lover can be relieved of his problem by the simple expedient of pretending he never reached puberty. (Indeed, the latter problem might be amputated in a way the former could not.)

In summary, while none of the reasons cited for the counselor's reluctance to challenge his counselee morally seems to warrant the total neglect of ethics in a psychotherapeutic relationship, the issue of moralism does present the possibility that ethics and psychology are inevitably in some sort of conflict, a conflict which would be bound to complicate interpersonal relationships of all sorts, not simply those of the professional. My appeal for a more consistent moral witness in the healing relationship, while still justified, in that case would become an appeal to live with this conflict. My gut reaction, however, is to believe that the moral and spiritual geniuses of the race have not always been in such psychic conflict. A nonmoralistic morality and thus a life both psychologically whole and ethically sensitive are possible. The call for an ethically responsible therapy is not an invitation to inevitable distress.

In the following three chapters, I shall set forth initially two pure types for understanding the nature and function of morality, two basic images of man's relationship to moral values and their role in his life. The first is derived from theological ethics and involves what has been called the Three Uses of the Law. The second is taken from the field of psychotherapy and will examine the place of ethics and conscience in the healing process, as set forth in Freudian, Rogerian, and—to a lesser extent—behavior modification theory. Then we shall see whether these two types are theoretically or practically irreconcilable.

The traditional pastoral office, be it in the Roman Catholic confessional, the Protestant counseling ministry, or the catechetical role of either, is a classical example of invoking the moral law in human relationships, while psychotherapy is an obvious case of the healing relationship. The pastoral office and psychotherapy can stand for the two types we would reconcile; but first let us clearly distinguish between them, lest one simply be absorbed into the other—lest, for instance, the pastor become but a half-trained lay therapist and pastoral counseling merely psychological counseling done by a cleric.

Paul Tillich once spoke to this issue. "As a human being, the minister may or may not radiate healing forces on the parishioner, and as a human being, the psychotherapist may or may not exercise pastoral care on the patient. But the minister should not try to heal as his function, neither should the psychotherapist exercise pastoral care as his function. What may or may not be united in the person is separated with respect to the functions of experts."[8] The common factor in the pastoral office and psychotherapy is human relationships. The honest encounter of two people carries within it the seeds of salvation and healing. Psychotherapy and pastoral care converge because they represent productive use of interpersonal relations and, in this sense, are open to all of us. Indeed I woud stress the fact that the pastor or the therapist as persons may deliberately seek to heal or to mediate salvation. They are not trapped by their social roles. Nevertheless, as pure types each is distinguished as an "expert" in his own line. The differentiation of the pastoral and therapeutic identities comes from defining these realms of "expertise." I shall refer only to three aspects of such definitions: the goal, the context, and the area of expert knowledge.

The goal.—The goal or end toward which an activity is directed does much to determine the values by which the activity is governed. Hence, insofar as they strive for different goals, psychotherapy and pastoral care are governed by different standards or values.

Psychotherapy is designed to achieve the highest possible degree of mental health. This is the unquestioned good directing the activity of the therapist as expert. "In his therapeutic work," Heinz Hartmann has written, the therapist "will keep other values in abeyance and concentrate on the realization of one category of values only: health values."[9] He points out further that the therapist will continue his efforts to relieve neurotic suffering, regardless of whether or not this will result in a morally better person. It should be affirmed that most therapists as human beings—as opposed to experts—will on occasion interrupt therapy in response to other personal values. Nonetheless, psychotherapy per se is governed by health values.

There is of course no universally accepted definition of health, the description of mental health being culturally dependent. Behavior which treats dreams as literally true may be deemed normal in some cultures but psychotic in others. Even within a culture, definitions or tests of mental health vary. At one point in his career, Reich, for instance, felt that "the real test of the cure of a patient was his achievement of full orgastic potency."[10] Despite the inability to give a definitive interpretation of the word "health," it still possesses a real and practical meaning in human life, representing an important value. Moreover, it is necessary that there be a therapeutic relationship wherein health is the value sought, for obviously it is not considered the supreme value in the pastoral relationship. Otherwise, in our pursuit of salvation, we might possibly miss both legitimate levels of health and the criticism raised against our views of salvation by the existence of disease.[11]

In contrast, pastoral care is finally oriented toward mediating the saving grace of God; salvation, individual and corporate, is its goal. To be sure, the conceptualization of salvation exhibits variations at least as wide as those for health. Suffice it for our purposes to acknowledge a distinction between them. As seen in Western religious tradition, salvation exhibits an ambivalent relationship to health. Healing is seen in both Testaments as symbolic of the saving power of God, and the eschatological state of the redeemed is depicted as free from all bodily suffering. But this is not the supreme good at any time, nor is the present experience of disease, physical or mental, necessarily an indication of a personal fall from grace. (Neither is the failure to recover necessarily a sign of inadequate faith, a matter of considerable significance in the discussion of faith healing. Otherwise those not healed are plagued not only with disease but also with guilt for their "little faith.") Because it is a relative good, health—theologically speaking—may become a focus of idolatry. Thus Williams, while affirming the New Testament concern for health, reminds us that "the Christian ideal of life envisions something higher than freedom from anguish, or invulnerability to its ravages."[12] Similarly, Oates warns us against "a religion that shapes itself around human needs rather than calling for a transformation of human nature into a new creation."[13] The psychologically trained cleric can easily drift into the near equation of mental health with salvation. The latter, however, inevitably involves sanctification and moral reformation, a fact of significance for our study.

Some years ago I read a report of the "successful" treatment of homosexuals. The patients, all young men with a strong homosexual drive, were brought in for treatment because of their history of recruiting partners rather openly at certain public places. Success was established by the fact that they no longer exhibited such behavior, thereafter manifesting great skill in recruiting ever new heterosexual partners. One might suspect that whatever the judgment of their progress therapeutically, measured against the standards of salvation the patients had simply changed to a more socially acceptable form of sin. Needless to say, the results of treatment would be judged differently depending upon one's image of wholeness.

The context.—Psychotherapy and pastoral care both take place within a context. Each is part of a larger role structure which adds a further dimension of meaning to the more specific roles of the cleric and therapist. The pastoral office is probably more profoundly affected by this element than is the therapeutic, but it is a factor in all helping encounters. The type of interpersonal relationship established, the kind of problems raised, and the significance attached to such problems will all be influenced by the counselee's understanding of the context as well as by the nature of the specific role participants. When someone goes to a psychiatrist because of a deep sense of guilt, he has obviously already judged it—at least to some degree—a matter of psychopathology.

If a man or woman says, "I hate my mother," and is reassured by the counselor, "That's OK; it is all right to hate your mother," what is the meaning of this transaction? If both parties understand this dialogue entirely within a psychotherapeutic context, the exchange may mean that the counselee is aware of strongly hostile feelings against the mother and that the therapist is granting assurance that these will not disrupt the counseling relationship, in that it is important to become aware of such sentiments. If, however, the client looks upon the counselor as a reference point for ethical discriminations, then the verbal messages may take on a radically different import. The counselee may have begun with a confession of sin, only to be informed that what he confesses is no longer categorized as sinful, an assertion which neither might really be willing to accept. The difficulty, of course, is that in a counseling situation the expert is so often invested with almost universal authority and wisdom by the suppliant that the latter may blur this distinction badly, even though the counselor himself may be quite clear about the context in which he is functioning.

The area of expert knowledge.—Both the therapist and the pastor must reduce the total reality of the encounter to some manageable scheme in terms of which it can be comprehended. The therapist *as expert* uses theory—psychiatric, psychological, social work, etc., depending upon his particular background; the cleric *as expert* turns to theology. Grave misunderstandings arise, of course, if either one forgets that his abstraction has automatically lost something of the full, personal reality involved.

The pastor, by nature of his calling, gives himself to the study of the community's witness to the revelation of God, including His moral will. In his pastoral office he gains further insight as he seeks to accompany his parishioners in their quest for the meaning of life, for the values by which to direct their conduct, and for a sense of forgiveness for lives less than they should be. Finally, he pursues a personal quest for God, striving to make the theology of the church his theology. Apart from such activity, the cleric has no expert knowledge; on the basis of such activity, he has a unique and meaningful function.

The therapist, by nature of his vocation, devotes himself to the study of the therapeutic community's experience in relieving the dysfunction of distressed persons. As he accompanies his clients through their odysseys, he gains a personal grasp of the theoretical descriptions of mental disease and the processes of healing. Apart from this area, the therapist has no expert knowledge.

Let me hasten to say yet again that the problems facing people cannot be neatly divided into those which are psychological and those which are spiritual. Thus both pastor and therapist are often better equipped to function if they possess some comprehension of the other's expert knowledge. Insofar as the parishioner conceptualizes his difficulties in psychological terms, the pastor will be aided to the degree that he has some grasp of such modes of expression. It is helpful, for example, if the cleric realizes that his counselee is not necessarily referring directly to his mother or father when he alludes to the tyranny of his "Critical Parent." Furthermore, he needs to realize that the paranoid is not assisted by his own well-meaning expression of sympathy and consolation, that the grief-stricken mother's angry outcries against heaven may actually be both therapeutic and the valid beginning of a profound encounter with God. Love must be informed to be effective. Conversely, the therapist sometimes treats patients who show considerable religious content in their speech and behavior. If he would correctly identify the pathology within such expression, he must possess some knowledge of the theology which underlies the normal life of the patient's religious community. I recall a psychiatric interview with a young Greek immigrant who had lived in a monastery. His frequent use of Christ imagery was taken by the psychiatrist as a sign of illness, while others with a more theological background found it a fairly typical form of speech, given his cultural background. Moreover, in the context of therapy a patient may raise questions concerning ultimate meaning, the depth dimension of life or, theologically, of God. While the therapist may not feel qualified to deal with such issues or may find himself holding a theological position strongly at odds with the patient's and his community's, he should be sensitized to detect shifts in the focus of conversation so that he does not confuse the spiritual and the psychological. Finally, it is both therapeutically and morally wrong for the therapist to use his authority *as therapist* to push evangelically any particular theological position, whether pietism, liberal theism, or atheism.

One further assumption is made in the conduct of this study, one which I trust will be justified by the evidence assembled. Tillich mentioned that which is "united in the person" being "separated with respect to the function of experts." I have sought to clarify these separate realms of expertise through looking at the offices of pastor and therapist with their corresponding conceptual schemes in theology and psychological theory. What now of their being "united in the person"? While as expert, as the occupant of one particular role in society, I may self-consciously seek to fulfill only one function and interpret a situation in only one conceptual scheme, yet as a person, as a sensitive living human being, I inevitably respond more holistically, transgressing the narrow bounds of my expertise.

Let me illustrate this by reference to the traditional distinctions between fact and values.[14] Supposedly the scientist qua scientist is responsible only for elucidating the facts of a situation, the structure of a given substance, the effects of childhood traumas upon adult character, etc. He does not concern himself with questions of values: whether that substance should ever be manufactured, what character is desirable in adults. Indeed, as we shall see, Freud and Rogers each sought to develop therapeutic techniques which would elucidate the psychodynamic situation and give greater freedom to the self but would take no stand on questions of moral values. Yet I suggest that such an ideal is illusory, for the scientist is also a human being; he functions not only qua scientist but also qua person, and as such he is inevitably forced to think in terms of ends as well as means, values as well as facts. The rate constant for the nuclear reaction process, crucial to deciding the possibilities of an atomic bomb, could itself be called a neutral fact sought by the scientists in the Manhattan Project. However, the agreement to take part in such a project, whether deemed wise or foolish, morally justified or evil, involved important ethical judgments. In a similar way, the ethicist may seek to articulate valid goals and standards for human conduct, but he can hardly afford to ignore the "factual" givens of the situation. As already suggested, love must be informed—factually informed—to be effective. To neglect the facts in a situation of ethical choice is surely a moral failure. The U.S. Supreme Court decision ordering school desegregation was an assertion of a value, the principle of equal opportunity for all, but it rested upon social scientific data indicating that racially separate schooling was always unequal. Thus while the discussion of facts and values may theoretically be separated in terms of academic expertise, it is united in the person of the academic.

For us as human beings, then, in contrast to our specialized role in society, it is normal to respond to life in terms of both facts and values. But in order for such a response to be responsible, obviously we must develop some understanding of both the factual and evaluative dimensions of the situation. We must, in short, seek to conceptualize and examine both realms critically. The actions of the self as personal agent are of necessity guided by both detached "scientific" judgments of fact and personal judgments of value. All too often, of course, one or the other may be largely tacit and not carefully considered, but we should expect to find at least implicit understandings of both in any very extensive discussions of human nature.

Let us apply this to the specific realms of expertise distinguished in our discussion. The psychotherapist as psychotherapist concentrates upon psychological theory and seeks psychological goals which are tested by psychological standards. As such he is not concerned to elucidate and judge values by ethical standards. Yet if as a human being he must come to some understanding and commitment concerning them, then we shall expect to find at least tacit expression of ethical judgments in his writings. While psychological fact and theory will remain the primary focus—the self-conscious purpose—of his conceptualizations, a careful reflection upon his writings will usually disclose secondary foci, including basic moral interpretations. (We shall see reason to differentiate between Rogers and Freud, even as therapists, precisely on the basis of their implicit "theologies.") The fact that these interpretations have been developed by psychologists, self-consciously functioning as psychologists, is not grounds for their automatic dismissal. Indeed the psychologist, because he is in the first instance a human being who happens to be in psychology, may bring important insights to value questions precisely as a result of his special experiences in therapy. On the other hand, if he functions on the basis of only tacit, unexamined value judgments, he may also proffer a morally deficient anthropology. Similarly, while the primary focus for theological reflection is upon ultimate meanings and values understood in relation to God and His purposes, the theologian or cleric as person will naturally be guided by his understanding of the factual (including psychological) realities of the situation. Kierkegaard was a philosophical theologian, but he has been read with profit by many psychologists concerned about psychology. Conversely, unexamined and erroneous psychology can distort a theological image.

Now we shall set forth two primary images of our relation to moral values and their role in our life, the ethical and psychotherapeutic understandings of the nature and function of the conscience. This we shall elicit through the study of the theology and psychology of conscience, concentrating upon the primary focus of each. Thereafter, we shall search out the secondary foci in each, the tacit—at times even explicit—supplementary interpretations. We shall look specifically for the theology implied in our psychology and the psychology in our theology, finally being so bold as to assert that, by learning also from these secondary foci, we may find a way beyond the apparent conflict between ethics and therapy. Initially, however, we must allow the theologian to be a theologian, the psychologist a psychologist, yet seeking to bring them into fruitful confrontation.

17

2   The Three Uses of the Law
A Theological Understanding

Let us begin by reminding ourselves exactly what it means to speak of a *theological* understanding of man's relation to moral values. It works from within a perspective on the human situation derived from the quest for salvation. In other words, a theological description of the place of moral values does not deliberately seek to answer psychological questions such as how values are learned and incorporated or to what degree they enhance or restrict our psychological freedom. The theologian as theologian seeks to cast light upon the role of values within the plan of God. In particular, he explores the purpose and operation of Divine Law as it guides both individuals and the whole human race.

This situation notwithstanding, theologians are also people, and the theologian as person writes from within the context of general human experience. Thus from time to time we shall expect to find implicit psychological insights in his works. Although the focus of his attention may have been soteriological, his writings read from this other perspective, with another set of questions in mind, may illumine the therapeutic dimension as well. While the authors to be discussed are fundamentally concerned with the ethical and salvific role of the Law, their writings also speak—even if indirectly—of its psychological role. Both insights relate to the explicitly psychological descriptions of the next chapters.

We have already asked ourselves about moralism, whether it is possible to have a sensitive relation to moral values without suffering under a form of tyranny. Our theological understanding, then, must be one which deals with a diversity of response, and for this reason I have selected the doctrine of the Three Uses of the Law. Because of my own Protestant background, I am devoting myself to an exploration of this doctrine in the writings of John Calvin, Martin Luther, and Emil Brunner. The fundamental concepts involved, however, are not exclusively Protestant. Though the terminology may vary somewhat, they are also part of Roman Catholic tradition, being found in such basic works as St. Thomas's *Summa Theologica* and the contemporary treatise *The Law of Christ*, by Fr. Bernard Häring.

As used by these authors, the term "law" carries a wide range of meaning. It can denote law in the specific sense of the Ten Commandments or in the broad sense of the structures of justice and order which society has evolved. It can refer to the ethical dimension alone or can be widened to include ceremonial law. But in all instances it is regarded as ultimately grounded in the will of God—even though it may represent a distorted expression of that will—and therefore as a moral imperative.

Law and Unrepentant Humanity

The first two uses of the law function with respect to man as sinner, and law in this context is associated with the wrath of God. Calvin exchanges the order of the first two uses found in Luther and Brunner. I shall follow the order of Luther and Brunner because it represents more closely the sequence of events in the individual case. (Psychologically speaking, Luther's second use corresponds to an intensification of the first.)

The first function of the law is to act as a *restraint* upon sinful impulses. In Luther's words, "The first use, then, of laws is to bridle the wicked."[1] Law in this sense is the guardian of the communal order, making possible the preaching of the gospel and indeed of any form of stable social existence. In this context law carries a broad reference, including not only the biblical commandments but also the laws of nations. Brunner emphasizes that we live in a framework of orders or restraints, experiencing them in the form of established habits, social customs, and codified laws. Apart from a system of controls for the relationships within a society, life in community would be impossible for sinful man. But for the Christian such law is more than a sociological necessity; it is a gift from God. "*Lex* [law in its first use] forms part of the way in which God, at present, preserves life in the created order tainted by sin, it is His way of giving us life, and especially life with one another."[2] Such is the "civic" function of the law for Luther or the *usus politicus* for Brunner.

Both Brunner and Calvin distinguish another, more specific function for this law in the life of the "not yet regenerate." It preserves from the gross excesses of dissolute living those who have not yet received the Spirit of sanctification; moreover, it acts as a preparatory discipline in anticipation of the disciplined life of the regenerate. Hence Brunner can acknowledge also the

19

usus paedagogicus, the law as the teacher who brings us to Christ.

The second use of the law is to reveal the righteousness of God and, in this light, the sinfulness of man. This piercing revelation of divine righteousness, these authors suggest, lays bare the sham of our human righteousness; in the light of God's holiness our pride and confidence are swept away. The law which began as restraint now engenders *condemnation*. "While it shows God's righteousness, that is, the righteousness alone acceptable to God," Calvin writes, "it warns, informs, convicts, and lastly condemns, every man of his own unrightousness."[3] So also for Luther: "The proper office of the law is to lead us out of our tents and tabernacles, that is to say, from the quietness and security wherein we dwell, and from trusting in ourselves, and to bring us before the presence of God, to reveal his wrath unto us, and to set before us our sins."[4] For all three writers law in its second use is an intensification and deepening of its more limited civil use.

The law which was intended for our salvation has apparently become the occasion for sin and death. The spiritual pilgrimage of the unrepentant sinner seemingly terminates in this condemnation. For him the law has served its purpose in exposing his unwillingness to acknowledge guilt, and to Calvin the searing reproach of his own conscience testifies to the justice of divine condemnation. For the children of God, Calvin's "elect," however, such judgment has a happier purpose, in that their terror before the wrath of God is not intended to leave them in despair or drive them to ruin. Its mission, rather, is to prepare the way for grace. Why therefore does God so chastise his children with this "hammer," the law? "To this end," replies Luther, "that we may have an entrance unto grace. So then the law is a minister that prepareth the way unto grace. For God is the God of the humble...."[5]

Calvin points out in a summary statement that the law serves as a tutor unto Christ in each of its first offices. For those who tend toward moral laxity, the law in its first use restrains passions which might otherwise lead them into gross degradation. Meanwhile, in its second function it serves to shatter the complacency of those who pride themselves on their moral achievements and who thereby make themselves unfit to experience the grace of God.

Although the purpose of these writers is to outline the

theological functions of the law, in fact they also present a psychological description of the individual's relation to the law, his motivations for obedience. According to Calvin, the unregenerate are aware—some more than others—"that they are not drawn to obey the law voluntarily, but impelled by a violent fear to do so against their will and despite their opposition to it." Even the children of God, as long as they are restrained by the law in its first use, obey from "the dread of divine vengeance."[6] Here too these writers recognize the instrumentality of secular structures. Insofar as the law restrains his outward activity, Luther confesses, "I do it not willingly or for the love of virtue but I fear the prison, the sword and the hangman."[7] Thus obedience achieved under the first use of the law reflects less reverence for its values than fear of the consequences of disobedience. Nor is the relationship markedly different for those assailed by law in its second function. The reprobates merely continue their angry defiance, and even those of the elect who pride themselves on their moral achievements and devotion to the law, when convicted by law in its second, more intense use, reveal the ambiguity of their allegiance.

Luther implies a further, extremely significant distinction within this negative motivation. In dealing with the law as a preparation for the gospel, he acknowledges that not all men move beyond the condemnation of law in its second use. The coming of Christ does not profit "the careless hypocrites, the wicked contemners of God, nor the desperate, which think that nothing else remaineth but terrors of the law which they feel."[8] The theological or second use of the law is an instrument of salvation, therefore, only to those who finally respect divine justice and have hope in divine mercy. The spiritual function of the law is redeeming only for those who—however ambiguously—have come also to love and honor God. This description, I believe, points to the psychological distinction between the negative motivations of simple fear and true guilt, a distinction which will prove to be vital. (We shall return to this, but meanwhile it is intriguing to observe its occurrence in this theological discussion.)

Law in the Life of Faith

Despite variations in order and phrasing, the three positions described above are basically the same. Agreement is not so immediately apparent, however, when we turn to a discussion of the third use of the law. In fact there are those who would question whether Luther even conceives of a third use. This problem but reflects our contemporary discussions of law and contextual ethics. It is significant, therefore, that we establish the appropriateness of all three uses of the law for both Luther and Calvin, representing as they do the two sides of this debate. Let us start with Calvin's account, since he clearly emphasizes this use of the law, indeed in some ways to the point of encouraging a legalistic interpretation of the Christian life.

(As we have seen, in the context of its first two uses, "law," while believed ultimately to be derived from the will of God, can yet refer in its immediate expression to social custom and convention. As pertains to its third use, "law" for each of our writers has to do specifically with the law of God revealed in Scripture, with law in the broader sense being intended to bring men and women to this more specific law.)

For Calvin, the third use of the law pertains to its function among believers. Even though the saint has been inwardly converted so that he longs to obey God's law, even though he has it written upon his heart, still he profits from the law in two ways.

To begin with, the law is the Christian's surest guide to the divine will. "Here is the best instrument," he writes, "for them to learn more thoroughly each day the nature of the Lord's will to which they aspire, and confirm them in the understanding of it."[9] The believer aspires to do the will of God, but apart from this divine instruction he will fail—even though he be free from sinful rebellion. Bound in the nexus of fallen humanity, man cannot perceive the true and perfect will of God without this divine leading of the law.

The second function of the law within the life of faith is exhortation. The believer needs not only its instruction but its constant and earnest admonition. Recognizing the old man of the flesh that remains in the faithful, Calvin writes most graphically, "The law is to the flesh like a whip to an idle and balky ass, to arouse it to work."[10] As with instruction, exhortation is inevitably required because of our involvement in sinful humanity.

So the law comes to the faithful as the fuller revelation of the divine will and as a source of divine exhortation. In keeping with the special place which Calvin assigns to the function of law in the life of faith, he also shows great esteem for its content. (In the catechism he calls the law the rule of life given to man by God.) Nevertheless, it would be unfair to the Reformer to imply that he sees the law simply as an impersonal code of conduct, a set of abstract regulations. Rather, law in its totality conveys a pattern for Christian identity, the image of the One whom we are called to follow. The law primarily reveals Christ and only by derivation a code. Christ is our law. "God the Father, as he has reconciled us to himself in his Christ . . . has in him stamped for us the likeness . . . to which he would have us conform. . . . Christ, through whom we return into favor with God, has been set before us as an example, whose pattern we ought to express in our life."[11] Thus the law in its instruction and exhortation is an instrument to lead us to Christ. Calvin emphasizes this conception of the law in his preface to the Genevan Bible which he entitles "Christ the End of the Law." The whole of Scripture (law in its broader yet religious sense) is intended to bring man to a personal knowledge of God in Christ.

In accordance with this high doctrine of the law, Calvin comes to regard the third use of the law as the "principal use, which pertains more closely to the proper purpose of the law."[12] Indeed all other uses are accidental. The divine commandments are intended to bring us to eternal life by leading us to the righteousness of God. But if, because of our sin, the law becomes the instrument of judgment and wrath, we must differentiate between such "incidental" results and the true character of the law. So after outlining the law in his *Instruction in Faith*, discussing its role before faith is born (i.e., the first two uses), Calvin begins his description of the Christian life with a section which he entitles "We are sanctified through faith in order to obey the law."[13] Here he clearly parts company with Luther and with modern contextualists.

Unlike Calvin, Luther does not recognize the third use of the law as its principal one nor as that most in keeping with its true nature. He sees the law acting in its primary function when judging, condemning, and terrifying the consciences of men, i.e., law in its first and second uses. Moreover, in some passages he specifically denies the relevance of the law for the life of faith. In his commentary on Galatians, Luther recognizes only a "double" use of the law, the first being civil and the second spiritual. He concludes his discussion of the second use by stating, "The law, when it is in its true sense, doth nothing else but reveal sin, engender wrath, accuse and terrify men, so that it bringeth them to the very brink of desperation. This is the proper use of the law, and *here it hath an end, and it ought to go no further.*"[14] Similarly, in his essay *Concerning Christian Liberty*, Luther questions the need for law in the life of faith. "It is clear then," he writes, "that to a Christian man his faith suffices for everything, and that he has no need of works for justification. But if he has no need of works, neither has he need of the law."[15] In some passages he actually speaks of the law and Christ being in conflict, saying that they cannot exist together. "Christ . . . is no Moses, no lawgiver, no tyrant."[16] (How interesting to note here the association of law with tyranny, a relationship we shall find in the writings of both Freud and Rogers!)

As Wingren has pointed out, Luther's ethics have a decidedly contextualist flavor.[17] Love shatters the restraining bonds of any law. "There is no law for the conduct of life," writes Wingren, "no law which can be learned as a future requirement or as a standard of saintliness, whereby the ethical life of 'the converted' can be guided into the right furrow."[18] Wingren repeatedly repudiates the tendency of Lutheran orthodoxy to teach a third use of the law which reduces Christian life and conduct to a code or scheme.

All of this, then, produces a sharp contrast between Luther and Calvin concerning the law in its third use. Nevertheless, I suggest that Luther does have a third use and that the contrast is really a matter of terminology and emphasis.

Luther used the term "law" largely as a correlate of active righteousness or justification by works as opposed to passive righteousness or justification by faith; for him it implied a code of ethical requirements to be met if one would avoid the wrath of God and so earn his way to heaven.[19] It was law in its first two uses. To be under such a law is obviously contrary to being under the gospel, grace, or Christ. When referring to that which Calvin called the third use of the law, Luther usually employed a term which did not carry the objectionable connotation conveyed to him by "law." The most frequent substitute was "commandment." In his two chief discussions of what is really a third use of the law, *The Greater Catechism* and *A Treatise concerning Good Works*, Luther regularly uses this terminology. Much of the apparent contrast with Calvin stems from this habit. (Luther is not scrupulously consistent in this practice. Sometimes he employs the term "law" in a context where a negative connotation is not implied. Hence he can write, "But to fulfil the law, is to do the things which the law commands with a joyful, glad and free heart.")[20] The contrast is further reduced when we remember that Luther's rejection of the law in the sense of justification by works is basic also to Calvin's theology. He too affirms the Christian's freedom from the law.

A real distinction remains, however, between the two Reformers, one which is reflected in this differing terminology. Luther's dark connotation of the word "law" emphasizes the Christian's repudiation of "active righteousness," with a corresponding emphasis upon freedom from the law.[21] Calvin's exalted connotation of the same word underscores its good and rightful place as a means of grace and thus the role of law in the life of faith.

Comparing their views on the Christian motivation for good works, we find another such contrast in emphasis. Luther stresses joy and freedom, while Calvin's accent falls upon duty. Consequently it seems only natural that Calvin would accentuate the third use of the law. On the other hand, if Luther, with his markedly more contextualist orientation, still affirms the necessity of the law (or, as he preferred, the commandment) in the life of faith, then the validity of this doctrine does not depend on repudiating contextual ethics. We are not tied to the noncontextualist position.[22]

Allowing for Luther's difference in emphasis, we discover that he teaches a third use of the law essentially the same as Calvin's. In *A Treatise concerning Good Works* and *The Greater Catechism* he presents this in considerable detail. Each of these works offers an exposition of the Ten Commandments as guidance for the Christian life. In the *Treatise*, Luther begins by asserting their importance in guiding men to the will of God. "We are to know, first of all, that nothing is a good work but that which God has commanded: and again, that nothing is sin, but that which God has prohibited and forbidden. And therefore, we have need of nothing else unto the understanding and doing of good works, than a knowledge of the commandments of God."[23] As with Calvin, then, Luther stresses law as a necessary source of guidance even in the life of faith. Moreover, he recognizes its exhortatory role. It is a scourge to complacency. When the faithful come to feel that they no longer have any sin or temptation, they need but look in the mirror of the Ten Commandments to find their weakness and see that for which they should strive.[24] Finally, Luther—with Calvin—asserts that the real meaning of the law moves us beyond any code of ethics. He affirms that Christ is the true content of the law, so that the fulfillment of it involves an imitation of Him, the evolution of a Christlike identity. In his sermon "Concerning Good Works, the Fruits of Faith," for example, he declares that we put on Christ in two ways: first of all "when we are clothed with his righteousness, which is done by faith," but equally though subsequently "when we weigh and consider that he is given to us, also instead of an example."[25]

As with the previous functions, the discussion of the third use of the law by the Reformers contains a description of the individual's psychological relation to the law's demand. The motivation for obedience in the life of faith contrasts with that pertaining to the first uses. Obedience is no longer achieved merely by the threat of punishment; it is desired for its own sake. "Consciences observe the law," Calvin writes, "not as if constrained by the necessity of the law, but ... freed from the law's yoke they willingly obey God's law."[26] Luther too emphasizes the change from the reluctant or compelled obedience, characteristic of the first uses, to that of willing obedience. "But to fulfil the law, is to do the things which the law commands with a joyful, glad and free heart; that is, spontaneously and willingly to live under God, and do good works, as though there were no law at all."[27] The psychological relation to the moral authority of the law in the life of faith represents a transformation of the inner man, and this new creation is the work of the Spirit.

The Third Use of the Law in Brunner
Fundamentally, Brunner's position on the third use of the law is a blend of Luther and Calvin. With both writers, he recognizes the

necessity of divine guidance in the life of faith. He would also affirm the transformation of the individual's psychological relationship from fear to aspiration. The law "is no longer the command of the Lord to the slave but the instruction of the father to the son."[28] He tends toward a contextualist interpretation of Christian obedience, distinguishing between the "Divine Command" and the "law" in terms reminiscent of Luther. But like Calvin, he affirms that the law is part of the context within which decision is made. We are guided by the Spirit, Brunner admits, but the Spirit speaks through the law, for few of us are so filled with grace that we can trust our spontaneous responses. Thus while the law cannot render decision in advance, it is relevant in advance of decision. "Whatever I can determine beforehand from the principle of love for a definite situation in life must be illuminating for me in the concrete instance of decision, it ought to direct me towards the Divine Command itself."[29]

In *The Divine Imperative* Brunner offers a useful addition to our understanding of the third use of the law. He suggests that the threefold function of the law expresses itself again as a threefold division within the third use of the law.[30]

Lex, law in its first use, expresses itself in the life of faith as a call to ordinary morality, to an expression of "the humdrum civic virtues." The standards of conduct expected of a decent citizen remain relevant for those who have been liberated from the law. Civic virtues may be suspect in the penetrating light of radical law (law in its second use)—even the devil would be a gentleman in England—yet theirs is still a valid, if limited, function. Even when seen in the light of faith, *Lex* remains a divine gift and a necessity for stable community existence. Because Brunner's ethics place a high value upon social order, he can argue that the Christian should forget the meaning of love if this is needed for society. It is outside the scope of our study to evaluate this emphasis or to examine the conflict between official duty—say, in condemning as a judge—and Christian love. We note only Brunner's recognition, within the life of faith, of the value of legalistic obedience to an ethical code, obedience accepted willingly from within the prior experience of Christian freedom.

Radical law continues as the "complete renunciation of all claims to 'virtue.' "[31] The Christian realizes that behind civic virtues is the law of God which demands perfect love, the sum total of all virtues. Thus he continually despairs of his own virtue and the purity of his will. His is the constant call to repentance, but it is a repentance within faith which far transcends the madness or passive resignation of despair without faith.

Finally, there is what we might describe as the law of faith in the life of faith. Here Brunner acknowledges the dual activities of exhortation and guidance as described by Calvin. When exhortation, the law comes as an urgent, concrete imperative for moral growth, as a call to strive for perfection, even though it is beyond us in this world. When guidance, the law of faith finds its opportunity in personal dealings, in that element of all relationships which goes beyond office and duty. At this juncture the Christian is most truly free to be a son of God. "The Believer's most important duty ... always remains that of pouring the vitality of love into the necessarily rigid forms of the order."[32]

A Review of the Theological Understanding

Whether the moral demand is experienced as the codified law of God or as the Divine Command known only in the context of decision, and whether it is confronted in the form of some external authority or known internally in the voice of conscience, its role as the moral values to which an individual must respond is not altered. In describing the functions of law in human life, these three writers were fundamentally formulating a theological understanding with which to answer theological, and in that context ethical, questions. While doing so, however, they also provided a fully human description which can be interpreted psychologically. We shall remind ourselves of the latter first.

Psychologically, their account distinguishes two basic relationships:

1. The first of these is characterized by resistance to the claims of the presented moral standards, as when one exhibits open rebellion or an unwilling compliance, dictated by fear of the consequences of disobedience. This is the situation in the first two uses of the law.

Some evidence exists for a further differentiation of this negative relationship. Each of our theologians recognizes two possible responses to the intensification of this antagonism, as experienced in the second use of the law. Theologically, this is explicable in terms of the activity of the Holy Spirit and man's acceptance or rejection of grace. But since this is a human experience, it is possible to give a psychological description of this distinction as well. Luther suggests that, whenever a man despises God's law and denies His love, that man's negative relation to moral authority remains unaltered by the "spiritual" use of the law. This extreme negative relationship corrsponds to the situation wherein the individual wholeheartedly hates and rejects some experienced claim of value, together with the one presenting the claim. But Luther recognizes—by implication—a not so wholehearted rejection of ethical standards. The law in its "spiritual" function opens the way of faith for those who both accept and reject God's law, who both love and hate their Creator. This second negative response to moral values differs from the first in its inherent ambivalence marking the relationship. Here the individual acknowledges the validity of the moral claim even though he rebels against it; he honors the one whom he opposes. Psychologically, the latter situation corresponds, I believe, to the character of true moral guilt; the former, to the character of fear which is amoral.

2. Finally, in the second basic relationship, this model distinguishes the man who freely accepts the claims of presented moral standards. His motivation is basically positive; it is aspiration. The consequences of failing to pursue such values are of secondary importance. Such is the situation corresponding to the third use of the law.

A further psychological characterization of conscience is suggested in this understanding. The incorporation of moral values psychologically means the evolution of a personal identity. To be sure, our writers do not detail all the ramifications of this fact. In Brunner and Luther, however, the emphasis upon personal response or decision in context would imply recognition of the fact that a moral decision is a response of the whole individual and not merely an expression of incorporated rules. Equally, the interpretation of the law as pointing to Christ and of the Christian life as an imitation of Him would suggest that moral growth involves the development of a Christlike identity.

Whether or not the Reformers prove to be psychologically

correct, their primary intention was to develop a theology of the moral life, to outline the role of man's various relations to moral values within the divine plan for salvation. In this context, even unwilling compliance with the demands of moral values, practiced in the negative psychological relationship, serves a legitimate function. It acts as a restraint upon immoral behavior and thereby preserves a modicum of social order. Apart from such restriction, communal life, including all the higher forms of ethical and religious behavior, is endangered. Love is freer to function in a just and stable order. Negative obedience, furthermore, carries within it the potential to be an instrument of divine grace. The love and mercy of God cannot be fully grasped until man takes seriously the claims of divine righteousness. Hence the heightening of his moral anguish may open the way to faith. Moreover, the law of God is a source of guidance and exhortation to those who live by faith, who live in willing obedience. Since human conduct is motivated—in part—by the free response to values, it is important, from the Christian point of view, that such values be in accord with the will of God. The human conscience, therefore, requires an external reference in Divine Law.

As suggested by Brunner, the conscience of faith or the positive conscience is itself threefold. The simple obedience of the negative conscience continues in the Christian's compliance with ethical codes, a compliance which is legalistic and formal for the sake of order and justice but which is also freely accepted as a response of faith and love. Then, too, the heightening of the negative conscience for the Christian is a constant reminder of his own sin and of God's mercy. The positive conscience, however, contains the individual's deepest values through which he continually aspires toward moral growth and by which he is directed in his unique and most personal responses to life.

Consequently our theological understanding records a complex picture, admitting several concurrent relationships between the individual and moral standards. In turning to psychotherapeutic theory and practice, we shall find a conscious effort to examine the psychodynamics of morality and in particular the role of moral values when internalized to form the conscience.

3   Moral Confrontation in Psychotherapy
Theory and Practice

Modern psychology and psychotherapy divide roughly into three general approaches: behaviorism, depth psychology, and humanistic psychology. The first traces back to Pavlov's classic work on conditioned responses in dogs and is essentially a learning theory. J. B. Watson saw in this a psychology free from subjective judgments, based solely upon objectively observable behavior, and coined the term "behaviorism." Perhaps the best-known contemporary exponent of the position is B. F. Skinner. The seminal figure in depth psychology is of course Freud, who charged nineteenth-century psychology with overestimating the rational nature of man. He saw our consciousness set precariously atop the unconscious, a vast, seething caldron of irrational impulses. Though differing from him in many key points, Jung, Adler, and the so-called neo-Freudians, including Erikson, share many of these basic assumptions. Humanistic psychology or the third force, as it is often called, is the latest of the three movements and represents a deliberate rejection of certain elements in the other two. It attacked behaviorism for being a psychology which failed to treat persons as persons and thus could not produce a psychology of personhood. It found in depth psychology excessive emphasis upon the unconscious and irrational together with a mistaken assumption that one should understand mental health in terms of mental illness. In contrast, it chooses to study normal, healthy, and superior persons, not the neurotic and infantile. Abraham Maslow, Gordon Allport, and Carl Rogers are three of the major figures in this movement.

For our purposes it is not necessary to decide which of these schools is "correct." Indeed it might be unwise to make such judgments; theories should be judged instead as being more or less useful. Donald Hebb, himself a behaviorist, has written, "A man who constructs a theory is certainly trying to hit on the truth, but the function of theory is better seen ... as a sophisticated statement of ignorance.... The function of theory is to guide us to new observations and better experiments. If it does this it is good, whether it is 'true' or not."[1] In their *Theories of Personality*, Hall and Lindzey remark that the acceptance or rejection of a theory "is determined by its *utility*, not by its truth or falsity."[2] In this sense each of the three schools is acceptable in that each provides a mode of interpretation which has been useful in experimentation and—of more import to us—in guiding the practice of psychotherapy. The mentally ill have been assisted to greater health by therapists who work from each of these perspectives, and each is able to employ its theoretical framework to explain the others' success. In the following discussion, our attention will focus upon the psychoanalytic and humanistic understandings, initially in the work of Freud and Rogers. This does not reflect a judgment that such therapies are always or usually more effective than a behavioral approach but, rather, that the crucial questions for our study have been asked more directly in the latter two schools.

Moral Values and Behavior Modification

As indicated, I shall be very brief in my treatment of behavior modification.[3] Though based upon behaviorism, behavior modification appeared upon the scene as a recognized approach only as a result of a growing disenchantment with talking psychotherapies. Beginning with the work of H. J. Eysenck in the early 1950s, doubts were raised as to whether patients thus treated actually improved faster or more permanently than those given no treatment at all. The opening presented itself for the development of new forms of therapy, turning in particular to Skinner's work on the experimental analysis of behavior. Behaviorism is basically a learning theory; behavior modification interprets the therapeutic process as essentially one of "unlearning" bad patterns of behavior and substituting better ones. Expressed perhaps too simply, learning theory asserts that one tends to continue behavior which is rewarded and to avoid behavior which is not rewarded or, endeavoring even more strenuously, to abandon activities which are punished. Therapy, then, consists of a careful use of reward and punishment to achieve desired changes. Moreover, these changes must be operationally definable, so that actual measurements of progress can be made. For example, the problem child is disrupting the class more or less than before; a simple count of the number and length of the interruptions can be recorded.

Activity, in this understanding, is a function of rewards and punishments. Undesirable conduct, it is argued, is often sustained, because unintentionally it is being rewarded. Our noisy child's unruly behavior is reinforced by the teacher; he is given added attention. In this situation, improvement could be achieved simply by terminating the reward. The teacher would ignore the behavior, making it less attractive. The initial response would probably be an increase in activity, but continued lack of response would lead to gradual extinction. The rate of progress would be further increased if the teacher begins to reward instances of desired conduct. He might heap praise upon the child when he acts with decorum. In many cases rewards are quite openly offered for specified behavior. A withdrawn patient who enjoys watching television may be granted additional viewing privileges in proportion to his time voluntarily spent conversing with others. To be sure, this approach may occasionally produce comic results. A friend of mine practiced this technique in the toilet training of his child. Every time she performed properly she received lavish praise. "There may be some drawbacks to this approach," he admitted, after going home one day to find his daughter seated on the throne, surrounded by all her playmates. She would not perform unless assured of an appreciative audience.

In contrast, one may deliberately set out to punish unwanted behavior or, using a more euphemistic term, respond to it with negative reinforcement. The chronic bed wetter has his mattress wired, causing an alarm to shatter his sleep if he relaxes his sphincter control. The homosexual receives an electric shock every time he is shown a picture of a nude male, so that he eventually develops an aversion to such stimuli. The alcoholic, after being chemically treated, finds himself averse to liquor.

Another variant, termed systematic desensitization, is employed especially in the case of phobias. Here the patient has developed an anxiety reaction to a stimulus which, viewed objectively, should not cause such terror. The fear of cats, of flying, of small closed rooms, or of sexual intercourse might be typical examples. In these cases, the patient is deliberately exposed to situations ever more closely approximating that which causes anxiety. He is given materials to hold which are increasingly similar to cat's fur, ending perhaps with a small docile kitten. Or he is made to imagine that he is on a plane, eventually being taken on a model of an aircraft, complete with sound effects, but he is taught relaxation techniques throughout. By such means the threatening stimuli lose their power to produce an anxiety reaction.

It may be observed that the foregoing sounds very much like the description of a technique, not an account of how a person decides what he or she will do. But this is precisely the point of the behaviorist school. What is available both to be observed and to be controlled are external conditions and responses, not intrapsychic states. Let me quote Skinner at length here.

> In each case we have a causal chain consisting of three links: (1) an operation performed upon the organism from without—for example, water deprivation; (2) an inner condition—for example, physiological or psychic thirst; and (3) a kind of behavior—for example, drinking. Independent information about the second link would obviously permit us to predict the third without recourse to the first. It would be a preferred type of variable because it would be non-historic; the first link may lie in the past history of the organism, but the second is a current condition. Direct information about the second link is, however, seldom, if ever, available. Sometimes we infer the second link from the third: an animal is judged to be thirsty if it drinks. In that case, the explanation is spurious. Sometimes we infer the second link from the first: an animal is said to be thirsty if it has not drunk for a long time. In that case, we obviously cannot dispense with the history.
>
> The second link is useless in the *control* of behavior unless we can manipulate it. At the moment we have no way of directly altering neural processes at the appropriate moments in the life of a behaving organism, nor has any way been discovered to alter a psychic process.... The objection to inner states is not that they do not exist, but that they are not relevant in a functional analysis.[4]

Thus behavior modification as a therapeutic procedure operates not so much by understanding what is going on in the patient (the desire for love and security, fear of a castrating mother, etc.) as by clearly defining the behavior to be terminated or fostered. In a sense, it leaves unexamined the meaning of the behavior to the patient. Our unruly schoolboy may be acting up because he has an extreme and unhealthy need for attention. To define health as decorous classroom behavior, achieved by ignoring his ill-mannered interruptions while lavishing praise upon preferred conduct, may be to leave untreated the more basic problem of his pathological need for attention. He has simply found a new way to be the center of things. On the other hand, there may be circumstances in which such a quest for inner meaning is either unnecessary or a luxury we cannot afford. It would probably be sufficient in most cases to assist a patient over a fear of cats without delving into their meaning to him or the origin of his phobia. In practice, the teacher may not have the time to engage in a depth encounter with our boisterous boy. Given his primary task, the creation of order sufficient for effective teaching is an understandable goal. (In anticipation, the reader may see here some parallel to the first use of the law in our theological understanding.) Moreover, both psychoanalysts and third force therapists acknowledge the reality of patients too withdrawn to engage in effective verbal therapy. In such cases, behavior modification may be the only recourse.

What then of the question of values and the moral imperative in such therapy? (I leave aside here as a totally different issue—though an extremely important one—the ethical problems raised in any form of manipulative treatment.) Strictly speaking, the issue of moralism cannot arise within a behavior modification framework. The term designates a situation in which an individual interprets his ethical standards as a demand upon him which must be met in order to gain the right to be. The person plagued with a moralistic conscience can know no peace or security, no self-acceptance unless he has fulfilled the law. All of this, however, describes "inner states," internal responses to the moral code. Thus the issue of moralism belongs to Skinner's "second link" and falls outside the realm of behavioral theory. This does not mean, however, that a moralistic conscience may not be operative in the counselee. We might argue that were such questions asked, if one were to speculate upon the "second link," that person might reasonably assume that "values" incorporated in the behavior modification process would tend to become part of a moralistic conscience. After all, the homosexual gains the right to be, i.e., ceases to be afflicted with electrical shocks, only by fulfilling the moral law, i.e., only by losing interest in nude males. Our withdrawn patient is granted admission to the heaven of the television room only by the active righteousness of engaging others in conversation. Consequently, while behavior modification itself, as a conceptual scheme, cannot really deal with the question of moralism, yet as a mode of therapy—here countermanding the avowed purposes of both psychoanalysis and the third force—it tends to foster a moralistic quality in the conscience. The fact that it produces results which are often both personally and socially desirable suggests that there are times when moralistic obedience is salutary. (In this instance, we are dealing with moralism which arises out of the attitude of the lawgiver, namely, the therapist. We shall see subsequently that moralism may evolve entirely intrapersonally, i.e., out of attitudes within the individual quite apart from the stance taken by external authorities.)

In contrast to the self-image of the psychoanalyst or the humanistic therapist, the behavioral therapist can be said to make ethical demands quite openly upon his patients. "You must give up drinking!" "You must develop heterosexual preferences." Assuredly, he may deny that these are moral challenges; not all reformations laid upon his patients are really ethical struggles. Overcoming the fear of cats, though perhaps requiring considerable courage, hardly constitutes what one normally means by moral regeneration. Still others may debate whether or not homosexuality is properly defined as a moral weakness, though the decision itself is—to some degree—a moral one. To declare homosexuality an illness or even an acceptable sexual variant involves an ethical judgment. Where the condemned behavior is antisocial (theft, lying, assault, etc.), even if it is adjudged to be the result of psychopathology, the standards of behavior being imposed are clearly socioethical norms. Thus it can be argued that a great deal of behavior modification precisely entails making moral demands upon the patient. In some cases the demands—the moral goals—are chosen by the patient who seeks the therapist's help in reaching them. The homosexual may wish to change. In other circumstances, the decision is made by society, which then proceeds to seek therapeutic expertise in imposing its goals upon the patient. This is exemplified by mothers who bring their children to have their behavior problems "remedied." The crucial issue to the behavioral therapist is not whether he should make behavioral demands of his patients but the moral adequacy of the standards he would induce in them.[5] Let us note that making such demands does not per se prevent therapeutic success, at least as measured in behavior modification terms.

Although behavior modification does not provide a theoretical framework by which one can explore the psychodynamics of moralism, it has made some significant suggestions concerning the whole question of the moral challenge in psychotherapy. Turning now to a longer discussion of verbal therapies, we shall seek insights concerning the "second link," the "inner states" which establish the psychodynamic character of moralism.

Freud and the Burden of Moralism

Sigmund Freud was actively engaged in the development of psychoanalytic theory for about fifty years, and his writings extend to some forty volumes. Over that period there were naturally major shifts in his understanding. In particular, it is only with the development of ego psychology and the refinement of the earlier conscious-unconscious topography through the threefold structure of superego, ego, and id that the psychodynamics of moralism can really be set forth. (Even in the earlier period, however, the essential problem is identifiable.) For our purposes we need not be concerned over the perennial tension in Freud between physiology and psychology, between a biological and a social source for man's ethical standards; nor need we accept the dominant role he gives to human sexuality.

The majority of Freud's papers published during the 1890s focus on the problem of neurosis and especially on hysteria. His primary clinical observation was that hysterics had rejected some thought as incompatible with the dominant mass of ideas which characterized their consciousness or ego, thereby producing a "splitting of the contents of consciousness."[6] He asserted that for these women (note the male chauvinism in the term "hysteria") such ideas usually developed in association with sexual experiences and feelings, citing, for example, the case of a girl who disapproved of herself having romantic thoughts about a young man at the time she was caring for her infirm father.

The basic concept to emerge at this stage of Freud's

thought was that of "defense," wherein the ego or consciousness defends itself against the unacceptable. But one key issue was left undecided in this early writing, namely, under what conditions the attempt to thrust an unacceptable idea from the mind has pathological consequences.

In a subsequent paper, Freud took up the suggestions that "the symptoms of hysteria ... are determined by certain experiences of the patient's which operate traumatically...."[7] The resolute search for these traumatic scenes inevitably brought Freud, "with no preconceived opinion,"[8] to the realm of infantile sexual experiences. So convinced was he, he asserted that everyone who had not had such traumatic sexual experiences before puberty could not be disposed to hysteria. The pathological factor lay, therefore, in the association of the rejected ideas with the memories of early sexual experiences. "Obsessions," he wrote, for example, "are always reproaches re-emerging in a transmuted form under repression—reproaches which invariably relate to a sexual deed performed with pleasure in childhood."[9]

A crucial question for this study remained unanswered. Why does the initially pleasurable activity become a matter of reproach? Freud offered conscientiousness, shame, and self-distrust as symptoms of this changed attitude but gave no reason for their occurrence. In short, the basic question of value commitments was not faced, and so neurosis was seen only as a defense against the memory of real, traumatic experiences in the past.

A major shift in theory occurs with Freud's discovery that at least some of the alleged sexual traumas reported by his patients were products of their imagination. Such findings forced a swing in the etiology of neurosis from accidental to constitutional factors, from infantile sexual traumas to the infantilism of sexuality. Freud propounded his libido theory and the concept of psychosexual development: the famous oral, anal, and genital stages, with the phallic stage being added to the picture some years later. Morality enters the field via the curbing forces exerted against libidinal development, and psychopathology results from excessive or ill-timed interference with such development, "regression and fixation on infantile sexuality [being] the hallmark of neurosis."[10] In other words, rather than tracing neurosis to actual traumatic events—possibly, for example, encounters with a seductive governness—Freud thought of a natural developmental process involving man's sexual drive, a process which could unfortunately go wrong, leaving a psychic scar. The paramount issue remained unchanged. Pathology occurred because of moral restraints blocking the expression of psychic forces rising up within the individual. This basic quality of the moral life affirmed in Freud's early writings remained a fundamental assumption for Freudian theory. It was always seen as a defensive and restrictive or repressive entity. Morality was a gigantic "No!" finally experienced intrapsychically, and—if excessive—could cause the personal disintegration resulting from neurotic disorders.

The crucial feature of depth psychology was Freud's assertion that a major portion of this moral restraint operated unconsciously. Removed from conscious awareness, it tended to function in an automatic, legalistic manner, unchallenged by man's higher rational processes, unrefined by further moral experience and the specifics of the immediate situation. The young child who was admonished against his early sexual stirrings might live upon maturing under the tyranny of an unconscious law, resulting in guilt reactions associated with the most normal and moral of adult sexual feelings. The goal of psychotherapy became unearthing such repressed material under the guidance of the therapist, follo̶wed by a healthier resolution of the reactivated psychic conflict. In this picture moral restraint in toto was not deemed pathogenic, but merely excessive moral restraint—particularly when operating unconsciously.

Two major additions must be made to complete this basic outline of Freud's psychology of the moral life. One is the introduction of the superego as the internal moral agency, following upon the development of his ego psychology; the other, Freud's account of the powerful place of ambivalence in man's relation to moral values and moral authority figures. The latter concept had been discussed at length prior to World War I in his *Totem and Taboo*, but while the idea of some intrapsychic moral agency had been implied in much of Freud's earlier work, the concept of the superego per se was only introduced with the publication of *The Ego and the Id* in 1923. Moreover, in this work it was still not clearly differentiated from the ego ideal, a decidedly different entity (to which we shall return).

For the moment, let us refer to a later discussion found in *Civilization and Its Discontents*. The major problem faced here is the natural hostility of mankind as a threat to civilization. Control, Freud asserts, is partially achieved by the internalization of aggression; the destructive impulse is turned back against its source, the ego, through the agency of the superego, which rages against it. Having said this, he turns aside to the beginnings of the superego and of guilt, offering two explanatory schemes: an "environmental" theory and a "constitutional" one. In reconciling these two, he offers the clearest picture of the role of ambivalence in the superego.

The "environmental" theory—essentially that offered in the discussion of the Oedipus complex—states that initially the bad is whatever threatens the child with punishment or with loss of love from the powerful figures upon whom the helpless young one is dependent. At this stage true guilt does not exist; there is only "social anxiety." Guilt becomes a possibility when such external authority has been introjected, thereby creating the superego. Thus the superego represents the internalization of external restraints, and obedience is given out of fear just as the law (in its first use) is obeyed out of fear of divine wrath. In this context, ambivalence is expressed toward our moral standards, for we wish to violate them but, fearful of the consequences, deny having such feelings.

The "constitutional" theory begins with an observation that the more scrupulously one follows his conscience, the more severe it may become. This is particularly true, Freud asserts, of the renunciation of aggression. His explanation involves a complex, double identification. The parental authority becomes internalized in the form of the superego—as previously described. At another level, however, the child becomes identified with the superego while the parent takes the identity of the child's ego. Thus the rage of the superego against the ego can at this level represent the child's hostility toward his father (i.e., the child as superego rages against the father as ego). The severity of the superego is not a true guide, therefore, to the severity of the parental authorities, for the harshness of the latter is augmented by the child's own repressed hostility toward his parents, now expressed as superego hostility toward the ego. This observation has particular significance for our study, pointing to the fact that the character of the superego, or the conscience, reflects *intra*- as well as *inter*personal influences. Moralism, for example, can be a self-inflicted wound.

Both of these theories, Freud contends, have validity. He seeks to combine them in terms of a phylogenetic prototype, i.e., a source lying in the dim origins of the race. He invokes the image of Darwin's primitive horde, as he did in *Totem and Taboo*, producing essentially a psychoanalytic myth of the Fall. Freud pictures the primal father holding absolute authority and keeping all the women for himself until at last the sons rebel and murder him. The conspirators then become rivals for the same women and, in order to avoid mutual annihilation, deny themselves the women of the horde. Hence the erection of the incest prohibition. They also experience a longing for the father's protection, power, and authority and a consequent remorse for their deed. This combination of remorse and self-denial is the first occasion for the establishment of the superego. These effects persist in the race as the innate constitutional factor leading to the suppression of aggression and are coupled with the present-day environmental factor of parental prohibitions.

One question remains. The internalization of parental authorities is accomplished in cooperation with a constitutional factor, the latter being traced to our phylogenetic heritage. Where was the constitutional factor to bring about the internalization of the standards of the primal father or to cause the sons to turn their aggression against themselves? Freud admits that the constitutional factor and phylogenetic type merely push the question of the superego's origin further back into history.

Whence the source of the primal sense of guilt? Freud directs us to *ambivalence of emotion*.

> This remorse was the result of the very earliest primal ambivalence of feelings towards the father: the sons hated him, but they loved him too; after their hate against him had been satisfied by their aggressive acts, their love came to expression in their remorse about the deed, set up the superego identification with the father, gave it the father's power to punish as he would have done the aggression they had performed, and created the restrictions which should prevent a repetition of the deed.[11]

But having established primary love-hate ambivalence as the source of the superego, Freud could really dispense with his phylogenetic prototype, and some of his subsequent remarks virtually amount to this. "It is not really a decisive matter whether one has killed one's father or abstained from the deed; one must feel guilty in either case, for *guilt is the expression of the conflict of ambivalence*, the eternal struggle between eros and the destructive or death instinct."[12]

This combination of the "constitutional" and "environmental" theories for the genesis of the superego forms, in my opinion, Freud's most adequate discussion of this whole problem. The environmental theory incorporates the view that the basic standards and attitudes which form the foundation of the superego are derived from the environment, initially from the parents and subsequently from other authority figures. The constitutional theory points to the basic ambivalence which characterizes these relationships with authority figures. As a result of the unwanted restrictions imposed upon the child by these figures, the latter become objects of his aggression, although it is an aggression which cannot be expressed because of their power. But underlying this situation and prior to it is a child-parent relationship of love. It is this second factor, I believe, which marks the difference between mere fear and true guilt.

A child can internalize restrictions which are governed only by fear. His avoidance of the hot stove can become automatic and virtually unconscious. Similarly, in the so-called war neuroses, under the traumatic conditions of combat one may acquire a fear of aircraft, for example, which subsequently continues as a phobia, the basis of which is largely unconscious. But these are hardly moral categories, and the emotion is not guilt. Insofar as such motivation is included in the concept of superego, it savors of an amoral substratum which must be distinguished from truly moral categories. (One is forced to admit, however, that our theological model does not always distinguish between these two. The motivation in the first use of the law could be either guilt or fear. Thus it corresponds to the broader meaning of the superego.)

It is love which transforms fear into guilt. As expressed in Freud's constitutional theory, the child's love for his parents leads to feelings of guilt over his aggressive feelings toward them. I suggest that at another level, the child's positive feelings for these authority figures would involve a certain recognition of their demands as valid, as constituting real values for himself. We do not feel guilty for breaking rules imposed even by loved authority figures if we feel unreservedly that these restrictions are wrong. So the superego implies a second ambivalence, a tension between acceptance and rejection of a moral standard.[13]

In summary, the superego represents the internalization of parental standards which form a subfunction of the ego and which also stand over against it, judging it by such standards. This internalization is achieved by a series of identifications. Although the character of the superego is largely determined by primary identification with the parents, its content and form are augmented through the influence of later authority figures (such as teachers) and through the general impact of the culture. (Incidentally, the foregoing description fits equally well the ego ideal.) The distinctive nature of the superego is disclosed by analyzing its relations to authority figures and to the external standards out of which it has evolved. These relations, as interpreted by the child, are legalistic. Standards must be accepted and obeyed; otherwise the child risks the anger and punishment of the external authority, not to mention the loss of his love and protection. Thus the character of the superego is basically prohibitive and punitive. In terms of our theological model, the superego is an internalization of the relation to moral authority which is characterized in the first use of the law.

In the case of the superego, the relation to the moral authority from which it evolves is also marked by a dual ambivalence. The relation of the child to the authority figures is attended by both love and hate, an underlying foundation of love to which is added a hostile response to the imposed restriction. Furthermore, the individual's orientation toward the *moral standards* comprising the superego is ambivalent as well. He accepts the precepts as the legitimate and in some senses good demands of authority figures, yet the necessity of the threat of punishment would indicate that he seemingly rebels against them. This quality of ambivalence changes the character of the ego's dread of the superego from fear to guilt.

The factor I would emphasize is that for Freud the superego became the model for interpreting morality. As in earlier theory, the moral imperative was seen to be restrictive, threatening, and punitive, a demand which must be obeyed if one would escape the wrath to come, a wrath sometimes expressed simply as the loss of love and protection, at other times more dramatically as castration. Clearly it is an image tacitly assuming that morality means moralism and that these in excess give birth to mental disorder.

Rogers and the Burden of Moralism

When one moves from Freud to Rogers, he may at first feel that he has moved out of the realm of romantic speculation and mythology into quiet common sense. We hear no more about esoteric entities such as the Oedipus complex, the primal horde, the id, or libido. Rather, in keeping with the general tenor of the third force, attention is focused upon the normal, conscious mind. Moreover, Rogers offers less theoretical discussion concerning the structure of the psyche, choosing to concentrate essentially upon an understanding of therapy. Nevertheless, despite these major differences, his account echoes Freud's in identifying moralism as the basis of much psychic disorder. (Let it not be assumed that I am seeking to dismiss the significant differences between Freud and Rogers. There are, beyond all doubt, very important distinctions between the two, differences relevant to our discussion, to which we shall return shortly.) I would underline the fact that at the first basic level, Rogers is with Freud in fearing the pathogenic potential of morality.

A not insignificant clue to the interpretation of Rogers—in contrast to Freud—is found in the terminology chosen to designate their respective theories. Freud developed psychoanalysis; Rogers, client-centered therapy. Both were therapists in the first instance, but while Freud conceptualized the psychic structure and functioning, Rogers sought only to describe a process of therapy. The latter's concern to avoid moralism is expressed initially in the basic character of his therapeutic stance, often designated as nondirective counseling. Rogers saw this as a clear shift in approach. "One brief way of describing the change which has taken place in me is to say that in my early professional years I was asking the question, How can I treat, or cure, or change this person? Now I would phrase the question in this way: How can I provide a relationship which this person may use for his own personal growth?"[14] The major note of Rogerian therapy was the scrupulous refusal to dominate, to control or to direct the patient in any way. His task was to provide a liberating atmosphere in which the patient could do his own thing, become his true self. No covert moral pressure in the form of a selective acceptance of the client should be applied. The therapist "prizes the client in a total rather than a conditional way. By this I mean he does not simply accept the client when he is behaving in certain ways, and disapprove of him when he behaves in other ways."[15] Whereas psychoanalysis tended to speak of the etiology of neurosis, in alluding to a severe superego, client-centered therapy concentrated more upon the healing of neurosis in a nonmoralistic relationship. Freud, one might say, concentrated upon the genesis of mental illness, Rogers upon its exodus. For both the villain was moralism. Rogers rejected even the diagnostic interpretations of psychoanalysis because, while not a case of moralizing in the usual sense, they were evaluative; and all evaluative thinking, no matter how objectively accurate, assumes "a judgmental frame of mind" and views the client "as an object, rather than as a person, and to that extent respects him less as a person."[16] Diagnosis is an imposition of the therapist upon the patient and thus but another form of the problem. The therapist as expert becomes the locus of evaluation, with both psychological and social implications. "When the client perceives the locus of judgment and responsibility as clearly resting in the hands of the clinician, he is, in our judgment, further from therapeutic progress than when he came in."[17] This psychological loss of responsibility for oneself becomes even more significant when one considers "the long-range social implications . . . in the direction of the social control of the many by the few."[18] Rogers has written of the dangers of such control, seeing in Skinner's *Walden Two* not a paradise but a threat to true humanness.[19] Thus the client-centered therapist must be willing to leave the patient free to make any decisions whatever. "Only as the therapist is completely willing that *any* outcome, *any* direction, may be chosen"[20] does he allow for the full growth potential of the client.

Rogerian theory is by no means devoid of all attempts to

develop structural formulations regarding the psyche, but these are expressed in less esoteric terms than one finds in psychoanalysis. Concerning the question of moralism, Rogers speaks of the problems arising as a result of introjected values, designating them "conditions of worth," a phrase with a clearly moralistic flavor.

> A condition of worth arises when the positive regard of a significant other is conditional, when the individual feels that in some respects he is prized and in others not. Gradually this same attitude is assimilated into his own self-regard complex, and he values an experience positively or negatively solely because of these conditions of worth which he has taken over from others, not because the experience enhances or fails to enhance his organism.[21]

What we find here bears strong similarities to the Freudian account of the origins of the superego; an externally imposed demand, the violation of which causes anxiety, eventually becomes internalized. One's right to be, one's worth is conditional. As we could expect, therapeutic progress involves the movement "away from the compelling image of what [one] 'ought to be' ... absorbed so deeply from ... parents," "away from meeting expectations," "away from pleasing others."[22] For Rogers, the "fully functioning person," the ideal goal of therapy, "will have no *conditions of worth*" but, rather, "will *experience unconditional self-regard*."[23] Within this context, therapy consists in overcoming conditions of worth, thereby enabling the client to reappropriate those dimensions of himself which have been denied. Might we not readily transpose the following description into psychoanalytic jargon? "The therapist must ... concentrate on one purpose only; that of providing deep understanding and acceptance of the attitudes consciously held at this moment by the client as he explores step by step into the dangerous areas which he has been denying to consciousness."[24] Therapy, then, entails the recovery of the lost—lost dimensions of the self and of experience. Health means an "openness to experience" which is "the polar opposite to defensiveness,"[25] an openness to the whole self. With increasing health one

> can feel and be his sexual feelings, or his "lazy" feelings, or his hostile feelings, and the roof of the world does not fall in. The reason seems to be that the more he is able to

> permit these feelings to flow and to be in him, the more
> they take their appropriate place in the total harmony of
> his feelings. He discovers he has other feelings with which
> these mingle and find a balance. He feels loving and
> tender and considerate and cooperative, as well as hostile
> or lustful or angry.[26]

(One may note here the optimistic tone to this image of humanness, a matter for further consideration.) For the healthy, nothing
need be denied to awareness. Rogers's technical term here is
"congruence." "When self experiences are accurately symbolized,
and are included in the self-concept in this accurately symbolized
form, then the state is one of congruence of self and experience."[27] Despite some major differences between Rogers and
Freud in conceptualization and approach, they seem to offer—at
this first level—strongly similar pictures of the place of morality
in the genesis and exodus of mental disorder.

Another strong similarity (but also a significant difference)
relates to their tendency toward ethical emptiness. Precisely at the
moment in a human relationship when some form of ethical
witness would seem appropriate, they fall silent. Let me quote
Rogers at length.

> But is the therapist willing to give the client the full free-
> dom as to outcomes? Is he genuinely willing for the client
> to organize and direct his life? Is he willing for him to
> choose goals that are social or antisocial, moral or im-
> moral? If not, it seems doubtful that therapy will be a
> profound experience for the client. Even more difficult,
> is he willing for the client to choose regression rather than
> growth or maturity? to choose neuroticism rather than
> mental health? to choose to reject help rather than accept
> it? to choose death rather than life?[28]

At the very moment that the client faces "the choice of life and
good, or death and evil" (Deut. 30:15) his counselor, appealing to
therapeutic necessity, offers no moral witness. (To be sure, the
therapist's own right to be must not depend upon the client
choosing goodness and health. This is an issue to which we shall
return.) Here one cannot but note the analogy with Freud. The
analyst, Freud assured his readers, would not play the part of
mentor. He did not set out "to abolish the possibility of morbid
reactions, but to give the patient's ego freedom to choose one way

47

or the other."[29] The patient is free to select what he will, and the therapist's "conscience is not burdened whatever the outcome."[30] But surely there is a difference between the judgmental attitude toward the other which is the curse of moralism and the gracious sharing with another of those truths and values which one has found meaningful! Do we not fail at this point if we offer only silence? The therapeutic emphasis in Freud and Rogers tends toward a moral emptiness which neglects the whole question of legitimate moral commitments and the creation of a suitable ethical ideal. Philip Rieff has compared Freud's ethics (and we could now add Rogers) with those of Sartre.

> Nevertheless, the Freudian ethic may be liable to an indictment of ... nihilism. As a purely explanatory and scientific ideal, honesty has no content ... the freedom to choose must end in choice. Here, at the critical moment, the Freudian ethic of honesty ceases to be helpful.... In this final suspension, Freud's ethic resembles Sartre's existentialism ... after a long process of self-recuperation through lucidity, the Freudian choice may be not more humane but rather more arbitrary. One need not be self-deceived in order to act maliciously.[31]

There is one highly significant distinction, however, between the two. Rogers, because of his fundamental optimism concerning human nature, his belief that men would not "act maliciously," could hold such a position more consistently than Freud. The basic question for the therapist, according to Rogers, was whether he respected the right and capacity of the client for self-direction or whether he thought the latter's life was better when guided by his counselor.[32] His whole therapeutic theory and practice rested upon the assumption that "the individual has the capacity to guide, regulate and control himself, providing only that certain definable conditions exist."[33]

This major variation in emphasis deserves extensive development presently, but meanwhile, let us note that—for all his protestation—Rogers is offering a moral witness, one which may need to be challenged. For example, he quotes Maslow at length, approving his discussion of openness and acceptance of others.

> One does not complain about water because it is wet, nor about rocks because they are hard.... As the child looks out upon the world with wide, uncritical and innocent

eyes, simply noting and observing what is the case, without either arguing the matter or demanding that it be otherwise, so does the self-actualizing person look upon human nature in himself and in others.[34]

But does the self-actualizing person simply observe "what is the case" and make no demand that it be different? Would he contentedly observe Hitler, despising the Jews, consequently setting about his systematic program of genocide but make no effort to have it otherwise? Does this not confuse the courage-to-recognize-and-admit-what-is with the moral courage-to-demand-that-some-things-should-not-be? Nor is the problem solved, I would argue, by appealing to the difference between feelings and actions, pleading that one is really only expected to accept feelings, not the annihilation of a whole people. Rogers quotes with approval the insight reached by a client in therapy. "I realized moral judgment had nothing to do with how I felt, only with how I acted. It suddenly became clear that loving and hating, for example, are neither right nor wrong, they just are."[35] Yet the New Testament proclaims that "if a man looks on a woman with a lustful eye, he has already committed adultery with her in his heart" (Matt. 5:28). St. Paul warns that all sorts of "right actions" (even giving one's body to be burned) lose their moral import if they are done without love. Again, it is not my intent to argue for or against any particular ethic. I do insist, though, that the attitude one adopts toward his feelings is itself in part a moral judgment. To use one of Roger's own examples, the child's feelings of satisfaction when he hits his baby brother surely have a moral dimension. Would it not be a moral advance to become a person who takes no satisfaction out of hitting others, let alone a small child? Once again Rogers's concern for therapeutic acceptance has blurred the moral issue. We must distinguish between the psychological value of being open to or recognizing the feelings that exist within us and the ethical judgments concerning those feelings which mark moral growth or deterioration. The therapeutic "ethic of honesty" is really not an ethic at all but a psychological judgment concerning the processes of therapy, which, having been adopted as if it *were* an ethic, obscures the necessity to make a moral discrimination as well. The tension between psychology and ethics has evolved in part from this false equation of them. Yet here again is our basic problem: Can we make such moral judgments without destroying the salutary impact of acceptance?

Lest I be misunderstood, let me add another note. While distinguishing sharply between moral and psychological judgments, I would never deny the fact that psychological insight may influence ethical discriminations. To refrain totally from all aggressiveness, for instance, may in the light of therapeutic experience come to be seen not as shining virtue but as a sign of self-rejection, cowardice, or the denial of one's moral responsibility to self and others.

Freud and Rogers—a Fundamental Disagreement

But a moment ago we observed that Rogers could hold his stance of moral neutrality with greater consistency than Freud because of his more optimistic view of himan nature. For Rogers, the fully functioning individual has the innate capacity to weigh experience and make the morally correct decisions. Human nature is basically trustworthy.

> We do not need to ask who will socialize him, for one of his own deepest needs is for affiliation and communication with others. As he becomes more fully himself, he will become more realistically socialized. We do not need to ask who will control his aggressive impulses; for as he becomes more open to all of his impulses, his need to be liked by others and his tendency to give affection will be as strong as his impulses to strike out or to seize for himself. He will be aggressive in situations in which aggression is realistically appropriate, but there will be no runaway need for aggression.[36]

Thus the therapist who assists the client to such psychological maturity has no other task to perform. He can safely leave his client to make his own moral decisions. In terms of our theological account, there is no seeming need for a third use of the law. In nature free, mature humanity is good, wills the good, and can recognize the good. No teacher is required to give instruction in ethics. To be sure, Rogers is not naive. Nor is he asserting that the fully functioning individual is an instantaneous saint. "I would not want to give the impression that [my client] ... always makes sound choices," Rogers warns, only that "to be responsibly self-directing means that one chooses—and then learns from the consequences."[37] There is moral education, of course, but the mature individual can be left with experience as his only teacher.

Essentially Rogers, and with him the third force in general, tends to side with Rousseau against Hobbes. Man is basically good, and society corrupts him. Granted unimpeded development, human nature constitutes a natural harmony which selects those values and behaviors enhancing the organism and the self, "which *inevitably* involves the enhancement of other selves as well,"[38] as naturally as "the infant who at one moment values food and when satisfied is disgusted with it, at one moment values stimulation and soon after values only rest."[39] Here is indeed the noble savage. How does he fall from this state of grace? He falls under the impact of the civilizing forces of society. As naturally given, the human being would expand his awareness and experience in the movement from infancy to maturity, always open to the totality of that experience and, likewise, to the totality of the self, congruent, growing in his capacity to love and in his moral awareness. It is the refusal of the significant other to be equally totally accepting which creates in the child the disrupting conditions of worth. He discerns the approval and disapproval of his mother regarding specific behavior, turning these into approval and disapproval in general. The infant "comes to be guided in his behavior not by the degree to which an experience maintains or enhances the organism, but by the likelihood of receiving maternal love. . . . He cannot regard himself positively, as having worth, unless he lives in terms of these conditions."[40] It is such moral and quasi-moral demands of society that destroy the natural harmony of our humanness, leading to the defensiveness which blocks truly creative living. (Again, we need not assume that society or mothers are in themselves evil. It is the process of imposing our demands that leads to the human disorder.)

The picture in Freudian theory is radically different. Freud stands with Hobbes against Rousseau, proclaiming that mankind is anarchical and only restrained by the curbing forces of society. The psychoanalytic picture agrees with William Golding's image in *Lord of the Flies* rather than J. D. Salinger and *The Catcher in the Rye*. The problem lies at the very heart of our humanness. Initially for Freud this was a conflict between instincts, particularly sexual instincts, and civilization. Civilization rests upon the suppression of instincts, but for all its advantages, it is not achieved without significant cost. "Experience teaches that for most people there is a limit beyond which their constitution cannot comply with the demands of civilization. All who wish to reach a higher standard than their constitution will allow, fall victims to neurosis. It would have been better for them if they could have remained less 'perfect.' "[41] All of this notwithstanding, Freud's unrestricted, instinctual man was not an attractive figure. Despite the cost and Freud's very real fear that the renunciation of instinct—especially the aggressive instinct—might be placing a psychic burden upon the race which it could not carry, he consistently affirmed the absolute necessity for such curbs upon natural man. In *The Future of an Illusion* he asserted that society must be built upon such instinctual renunciation, without which the majority of mankind would not even engage in the minimal labor necessary to maintain life, "for the masses are lazy and unintelligent, they have no love for instinctual renunciation."[42] By accepting this bitter pill of renunciation, the greatest moral and social achievements are reached. Thus he states with pride that "the Jews imposed on themselves constantly increasing instinctual renunciation, and thereby reached . . . ethical heights that remained inaccessible to the other peoples of antiquity."[43] Given the innate conflict of instinct and civilization, the natural and the disciplined, body and spirit, the choice, however reluctantly, must be for spirit. "The harmonious development of spiritual and bodily activity—as achieved by the Greeks—was denied to the Jews. In this conflict their decision was at least made in favour of what is culturally the more important."[44] In the later Freud, of course, the nature of the human tragedy was revealed as the innate conflict between eros and death, the eternal struggle between the forces of life and growth and those of destruction and decay, manifest in the natural hostility between men. "The greatest obstacle to civilization," he wrote, is "the constitutional tendency in men to aggressions against one another."[45] The fateful question for the race was whether it could master "the derangements of communal life caused by the human instinct of aggression and self-destruction."[46] Regardless of the problems of moralism, for Freud the therapist there could be no question of outgrowing the need for moral guidance, for law in all its uses. Indeed, given what can only be described as a vision of fallen humanity, bereft of hope in God and thereby of grace, one might wonder if we ever move beyond the realm of law in its first use.

Here we see a fundamental clash of views between classical psychoanalytic theory and the third force. How optimistic or pessimistic should we be in our foundational image of human nature? At this point Freud and Rogers are in dispute not over the facts of individual case histories but over the ultimate context in which one sets such facts. (The situation is quite analogous to Rogers's dispute with Skinner over the latter's narrow determinism, which denies the whole area of human freedom and responsibility.) We are, I suggest, in the realm of ultimate images of humanness or what is called in some other circles theological anthropology. Neither theory is as theologically innocent as its advocates might like to pretend. It is an issue with considerable import for the whole question of the moral imperative in human relationships, yet I would hasten to add that we need not opt for the Freudian position in order to justify an ethical witness in therapy.

One further point. Freud and Rogers join hands again in their "theological anthropologies," with their basic naturalism. Rogers's hope for man lies in a *natural* harmony. We have already alluded to the fully functioning individual choosing a moral course as naturally as the child takes food. At yet another time he makes the analogy between the natural balance of impulses basic to our humanness and the character of the lion, that symbol of the "ravening beast" whose "various tendencies and urges have a harmony within him."[47] Just as natural to Freud is the basically conflicting character of man. Our problem is not a moral failure but an innate clash between instinct and civilization or, later, a clash between two instincts, eros and death. So Will Herberg comments that Freud offers us a variant of the doctrine of original sin, one tending toward a biologistic Manicheanism.[48] But as if in response to Rogers and Freud, writers as diverse as Allen Wheelis and Reinhold Niebuhr remind us in their various ways that it is the nature of mankind to transcend nature. There is no such thing as the purely natural expression of a human instinct or impulse. One always decides how to react to his nature. "To kill or to befriend are equally expressive of the nature of man. When one is designated right and the other wrong we have separated ourselves from nature, hold to a standard of our own making."[49] "The sexual, as every other physical impulse in man, is subject to and compounded with the freedom of man's spirit."[50] Because man can transcend himself, whatever one's judgment concerning the natural harmonies or conflicts within him, these do not entirely define the human situation. Man can choose how he will respond to the "givens" of his natural situation, and thereby he gains a moral capacity which transcends the natural. Consequently, whether one agrees with Freud or Rogers, the issue of moral choice remains.

In summary, setting aside behavior modification therapy, we see that, with their quite diverse views, Freud and Rogers nonetheless both warn us of the dangers of moralism in therapy. Given his more optimistic anthropology, Rogers is able to adopt a more consistent "hands-off" moral posture than Freud. Both, however, correctly point to the pathogenic potential in any moral confrontation, although Freud would see this as a cost which, tragically, must be met for the sake of society. Accepting the validity of much of what they say, we may still ask whether or not this exhausts the possibilities for moral psychodynamics. In the next chapter we shall examine some other facets of the psychology of conscience which open new possibilities for our consideration.

4   Further Reflections on
The Psychology of Conscience

Our discussion, it will be recalled, focuses on the apparent conflict between moral witness and the therapeutic efficacy of unconditional acceptance. Behavior modification clearly involves making moral and quasi-moral demands. If psychology and ethics are here in tension, a debate is prompted either about the ethics of the technique itself or the standards to be inculcated. With the schools of therapy illustrated by Freud and Rogers, the imposition of a moral challenge is seen to disrupt the freedom of the patient (including his freedom to be immoral) which is so necessary for providing a context within which psychological healing can take place. We cannot accept the client as he is and at the same time demand that he be other. Freud and Rogers, however, differ in their fundamental evaluation of mankind. The latter's optimism concerning mankind's innate moral harmony justifies, as he sees it, his consistent policy of moral nonintervention, whereas Freud's bleak image of humanness in conflict forces him to acknowledge the social necessity of moral intervention and instinctual renunciation. (There is, as it were, a split between Freud as therapist and Freud as citizen.) In either case therapy and ethics are in inevitable conflict.

A basic assumption in both accounts is that morality is unavoidably moralistic. The conscience for Freud became virtually identical with the superego, and as we have seen, this means it became both prohibitive and threatening. So enamored is it of the punitive that it may even permit moral transgressions in order to have the joy of inflicting retribution, a phenomenon which Franz Alexander terms the "corruptibility" of the superego.[1] Our relation to its standards is legalistic; they must be obeyed, or we suffer the anger and punishment of this internal judge. Though conceptualized in less dramatic language, morality as described by Rogers operates in an equally moralistic fashion. His scrupulous rejection of any "judgmental frame of mind" and his description of introjected values as "conditions of worth" clearly rest upon such an assumption. In both cases, morality reflects the general situation in the first use of the law. This analogy is made quite specific in Freud's discussion of the essential ambivalence marking the conscience. In some sense, one respects its standards but at the same time wishes to violate them. (This calls to mind those descriptions of Christian ethics which make the life of faith akin to a catalog of all the really neat things one must not do.) Before we seek to deal finally with the issue of moralism, we must examine whether this psychology of conscience is complete even in its own terms. Specifically, does one inevitably experience all moral values as an imposition, as an extraneous demand, or may such values not also be accepted as pointers to what one truly wishes to be?

As indicated in the previous chapter, Rogers focused upon the processes of therapy, while Freud sought to articulate the structure and function of the psyche. Not surprisingly, we find more concrete reflection upon the psychodynamics of conscience in the latter's work and shall therefore begin our search with the psychoanalytic literature, alluding subsequently to parallels in Rogers.

The Positive and Negative Consciences

If the superego is characterized by the introjection of standards derived from ambivalent relationships, one might naturally ask, "What about the possibility of conscience values arising from the introjection of unambivalent relationships?" As a matter of fact, there are two, one of which has already been mentioned in our discussion of fear and guilt. In this first instance, obedience is negatively motivated by the fear of punishment, and the authorities promoting such standards are pure objects of fear or hatred.

A second form of unambivalent relation to authority figures would be one which inspires only feelings of love or at any rate positive emotion. If the values presented by such authorities engender no opposition and incur no hostility, then we rightly assume that they are interpreted not as restrictions to be accepted or resisted but as values desirable in themselves, as goals freely sought. Such a relation to moral standards is of course analogous to that described under the third use of the law in our theological discussion. This unambivalently positive relation to moral standards and moral authorities, I contend, is more than a possibility; it is an actual, clinical entity described by Freud, one which he consistently underestimates. The name "ego ideal" properly belongs to the introjection of this second form of relationship and constitutes what I am calling the positive conscience, the super-ego being the heart of the negative conscience.

Freud's first detailed discussion of a moral and critical sub-function in the ego occurs in his paper "On Narcissism: An Intro-duction." In accounting for the repression of instincts, he postu-lates that man has "set up an *ideal* in himself by which he measures his actual ego."[2] During the course of this work, Freud discusses a wide range of topics, not all of which have a bearing on the subject of morality. Moreover, some references pertaining to his postulated moral subfunction have the characteristics of the superego. Nevertheless, the main emphasis of this account is on the exploration of narcissism or self-love as a useful category in psychoanalytic theory, and set within that context, his new entity—which he designates either as the "ideal ego" or the "ego-ideal"—is properly considered as the ego ideal.

> To this ideal ego is now directed the self-love which the real ego enjoyed in childhood. The narcissism seems to be now displaced on to this new ideal ego, which, like the infantile ego, deems itself the possessor of all perfec-tions.... That which he projects ahead of him as his ideal is merely his substitute for the lost narcissism of his child-hood—the time when he was his own ideal.[3]

As described here, the ego ideal is an object of love; it is desired. It is the image of the ideal self, and insofar as it is attained, the ego thereby achieves some of the unlimited self-respect which was the child's. The ego ideal is the ego as it wishes to be; it contains the requirements which the latter demands of itself as the price of acceptance. Therefore the primary emotion experienced in failure to achieve its standards would be not fear or guilt but self-rejection. The moral entity within the ego which Freud posits as heir to primary narcissism would indeed be an ego ideal and not a superego.

Some years later, in *Group Psychology and the Analysis of the Ego*, Freud dealt again with the subject of identification, dif-ferentiating between identification with the ego and identification with the ego ideal. Of particular interest is his description of the pre-Oedipal identification of the small boy with his father. One can safely assume that there is some identification of the child's ego with the father. The youngster openly imitates his parent, puts on his shoes or picks up his pipe and pretends that he is daddy. But Freud's account suggests that there is also identification with the ego ideal. "A little boy will exhibit a special interest in his father; he would like to grow like him and be like him, and take his place everywhere. We may say simply that he takes his father as his ideal."[4] The father becomes the pattern; he is an ideal ego. Although not dealing specifically with the issue, Freud's discussion clearly implies that the introjection of this relationship produces an entity distinct from the superego. Obviously there is a contrast between this early child-parent relationship and that existing in the Oedipal situation. Once the child regards him as a rival, Freud says, "his identification with his father then takes on a hostile colouring."[5] By implication, the pre-Oedipal relationship is not colored by hostility but presumably is one of a purely affectionate nature. Freud immediately denies this extreme conclusion, asserting that "identification, in fact, is ambivalent from the very first."[6] Yet he seems at times to be making a quantative difference which amounts to a qualitative one. Four years later he wrote, "As regards the prehistory of the Oedipus complex in boys, we are far from complete clarity. We know that that period includes an identification of an *affectionate* sort with the boy's father, an identification which is still *free from any sense of rivalry* in regard to his mother."[7] Even granting the improbability of any affectionate relationship which is not accompanied by some ambivalence, the pre-Oedipal situation described here would appear to involve such a low degree of this as to be qualitatively different from the relationship described in the Oedipus complex. Consequently its introjection would produce a moral entity qualitatively distinct from the superego, with characteristics such as we have attributed to the ego ideal. Once this entity and this relationship are conceded, we may assume that even in the Oedipal situation there will be facets of the parental personality and ethical standards to which the child relates in a largely affectionate and unambivalent manner (even then the boy will not hate or oppose everything about his father), and these will be incorporated into the ego ideal, not the superego.

In the period immediately following the publication of *The Ego and the Id*, the term "ego ideal" was dropped from Freud's works, except in a brief section in his 1932 *New Introductory Lectures on*

Psychoanalysis, where it had become a subfunction of the super-ego, roughly equivalent to the latter's ethical norms. This bias toward the equation of the conscience with the superego reflects many segments of Freud's own personality and life which we need not review here. Suffice it to say that this narrow understanding of the conscience does not accord fully with his own therapeutic experience. Indeed the ego ideal can be used to explain certain clinical observations made by Freud which he could not interpret adequately on the basis of the superego alone.

In 1931 Freud produced a paper, "Libidinal Types," in which he distinguished three main character formations, according to the disposition of the libido. The *erotic* type primarily invests the libido, its emotional energy, in the object; loving and being loved are of the greatest importance. The *obsessional* type is characterized by the supremacy of the superego. This person is governed by dread of conscience rather than the fear of losing love. Freud is forced to describe his third type, the *narcissistic*, mainly in negative terms: "There is no tension between the ego and super-ego—indeed, starting from this type one would hardly have arrived at the notion of a super-ego; there is no preponderance of erotic needs; the main interest is focused on self-preservation; the type is independent and not easily overawed."[8] I suggest that the narcissistic type could be described positively as being governed primarily by the ego ideal. Such people would be independent, subject neither to outer authorities nor to incorporated standards not immediately pleasing to them, i.e., to the superego. Clearly, if coupled with an ethically inadequate ideal, such extreme moral independence would provide the basis for a socially dangerous orientation of the self. All of this is in harmony with Freud's subsequent remark that the narcissistic individual's "mental composition also contains some essential conditioning factors which make for criminality."[9]

The differentiation of the ego ideal from the superego also casts light upon the subject of "successful" repression. If such success is achieved under the influence of the superego, then the associated ego ambivalence seemingly is not strong enough to produce any pathological effects in the form of symptoms or acting out. Yet this ambivalence would still be detectable in analysis. Despite this, Freud refers to clinical evidence for a more perfect form of successful repression. In some instances a repressed impulse "seems to *undergo complete destruction*, in which case its libido is finally diverted into other channels. I have suggested that this is what happens where the Oedipus complex is dealt with normally. In this desirable state of affairs, the Oedipus complex would thus not merely be repressed, but would be actually *destroyed in the id*."[10] If he really means a biological drive arising in the id, this will not be destroyed by any act of ethical renunciation. The destruction of an impulse here clearly refers to the disappearance of a desire which is the equivalent, in psychoanalytic terms, of diverting libido into a new channel. But we have seen that repression of an impulse or desire under the influence of the superego does not accomplish such full renunciation. The impulse retains its attraction for the ego. Its rejection is consequently undermined by ambivalence. The true disappearance of a desire would require its unambivalent rejection, which, I suggest, is equivalent to repression under the influence of the ego ideal.

In summary, Freud's ego psychology makes at least implicit use of the concept of the ego ideal as an entity distinct from the superego. A complete psychoanalytic theory allows for two orientations to moral authority: one pertaining to the superego and having the characteristics associated with the first use of the law, a second pertaining to the ego ideal and having the characteristics associated with the third use of the law.

Can we find in Rogers anything equivalent to the Freudian differentiation between the ego ideal and the superego, between the positive and negative conscience? Though its expression is often implicit rather than explicit, I believe the same distinction is discernible. We have noted in Freud that the move from repression under the superego to that under the ego ideal is salutary, leading to a more successful resolution of instinctual conflict. Similarly, in Rogers one reads that therapeutic progress involves a movement from imposed values to those which are more truly representative of the individual's own feelings, ones which are ego syntonic. "This study permits the conclusion that there is a change in the valuing process during therapy, and that one characteristic of this change is that the individual moves away from a state where his thinking, feeling, and behavior are governed by the judgments and expectations of others, and toward a state in which he relies upon his own experience for his values and standards."[11] In other works Rogers speaks about progress in therapy involving a movement away from pleasing others, away from doing those things a person *should* do rather than what he *wants* to do, and toward responsible self-direction.[12] Now there may be more here than simply a shift from the positive to the negative conscience. Health for Rogers, like Freud, also entailed escape from unconscious tyranny to conscious control or, in his terms, from distorted awareness to congruence. Yet there is equally something of the positive-negative conscience distinction, the contrast between imposed standards and self-chosen ends. This distinction is implicit in his suggestion that changing the locus of evaluation from others to the self involves overcoming conditions of worth.[13] Conditions of worth, it will be recalled, though ultimately derived from the demands placed upon the individual by others, are nonetheless internal in their point of operation, being equivalent to introjected values. Thus this alteration in the locus of values is really not only from external to internal judgment, from social anxiety to self-criticism; it also entails a change in the internal moral arbiter, from one carrying imposed standards to one expressive of the self's true moral aspirations, a shift from the negative to the postive conscience. (We shall have reason to question, however, whether this shift alone insures psychic health, quite apart from moral growth.)

*   *   *

For some period of my life, I served as chaplain at a large medical center, a position which provided an opportunity of relating to a wide cross section of people and observing, in some cases, the role of incorporated moral values in their lives. While the data gathered does not establish any clinical hypothesis concerning the role of values in the etiology of disease, it can help to clarify the issues raised in our discussion. The examples given here may make more concrete our (as yet) rather abstract psychological account.

When severe illness strikes, the operation of the negative conscience may find expression in the association of suffering with divine punishment, sickness with the Law of Talion. The patient may come to see illness as a form of retribution. A sixty-two-year-old woman with cancer of the colon had been in extreme pain for a protracted period by the time of her admission to hospital. Shortly afterward, she recounted some of the details to me.

Patient: I always visited my friends when they were sick, but I never knew how much pain they were having.

Chaplain: Sometimes makes you wonder why these things happen, doesn't it?

Patient: Well, I guess it is to make us nice.

Chaplain: How do you mean?

Patient: We get nasty so we have to get sick to make us nice. I never knew sickness before. Never took more than an aspirin. You could never say "hospital" to me. But they really got me this time.

(Such frank assertions that their diseases were manifestations of retribution usually appeared only in patients who were psychologically, if not physically, in extreme situations.) Eleven days later, this woman had come successfully through two operations; although weak, she was in little pain and well en route to recovery. Now, when discussing the reason for her illness, she referred only to a tumor of unknown origin. It might be, of course, that she had interpreted her operations as punishment, sufficient punishment to quiet her negative conscience.

Rebellion and anger can also be signs of the negative conscience. Patients in this category tend to accept the Talion principle as operative with respect to illness but deny that in their case such punishment represents justice. A sixty-one-year-old male patient remarked,

Sometimes I wonder, though, as I lie here looking around. (I have been here six weeks.) I have tried to be a good man, never deliberately did harm to anyone. My wife, she *is* good. Then I look around me and see lots of people I know who are no good. They do lots of things I wouldn't do, yet they seem to be happy and healthy.... I wonder is there an afterlife where we get the happiness they seem to enjoy and where they get what's coming. But I won't let it get me down.

The patient went on to discuss in detail an attempted robbery of his father-in-law's store. After a fight in which he had been slightly injured, the culprits were caught by police. This story had not been written up correctly in the papers. Again he pointed to injustice.

> Twelve months it took us to see that they got punished. We had to go to court twenty times before we could get them sent down for five to ten years, even though they were caught red-handed with guns and the money. Twelve months to get those hoodlums punished, and then they get out in four and a half years!... Makes you wonder; but I am not going to change; I'll stay good.

Obviously goodness in this instance conveyed not so much the idea of what he wholeheartedly wanted to be as a demand he accepted in order to avoid punishment or to gain a reward.

Finally, one may assume some involvement of the negative conscience where the patient reveals ambivalent allegiance to values which have become significant at the moment. A fifty-eight-year-old man had a cancerous growth removed from his neck. I revisited him on the day that he received a favorable post-operative report. He was expressing great relief and asking to make a donation to my work. The conversation turned to church attendance, a subject which the patient had raised earlier while nervously awaiting the results of his surgery. His ambivalence was apparent.

> As I told you, I was raised in the church. Then I got away from it and haven't been for some time. To tell the truth, I married a Catholic girl, and that really started it. I didn't go with her, but I never went anywhere. I know Father L. at the Protestant Episcopal church near my business. I talk to him quite a lot, but I don't go to church.... It is quite a problem with the different religions.... I have a son who is twenty-one. He is growing up just like me. [*Tears.*] He went to the Catholic church for a while but now he no longer goes. That is no good.... I've got two little girls. They are being raised very devout.... I can't understand the hold the Catholic church has on its people.... I wouldn't let any of my children go to parochial school. Let them go there, and you can never shake it out of them. I have three brothers-in-law. They can drink like fish. Money is no problem; they all make lots. Yet they are always drinking. They don't care what they do to people. They would do anything. They come out of mass and go to the tavern and get drunk if they want to. I can't stand being a hypocrite. If I believed, then I would live up to it.

It is quite understandable that an extreme crisis of health

is more apt to hook our negative than our positive conscience. Nevertheless, the disruption of disease carries with it the menace of cherished achievement being swept away or of desired goals not being reached. Illness thus represents a threat to the values of the positive conscience as well. It can endanger a cherished self-image.

The treatment of a fifty-seven-year-old married woman with cancer of the throat included surgery and a long course of radiation therapy, providing the opportunity for a continued relationship between us. She was a quiet, emotionally controlled lady who appeared to put a high value on personal competence. She liked to think of herself as one who could handle situations. Often she stressed her ability to face disease and physical suffering, how she could amaze the doctors with her toughness. "What a woman!" they would cry. Moreover, she clearly thought of herself as the strong member of the family. Early and frequently she raised the subject of her husband's recent retirement, asserting that *he* found it very difficult to adjust, even though *she had worked for two years preparing him for this change.* She had, in addition, been responsible for giving financial stability to the family. "My husband comes from a family of boys who never really took up their responsibilities," she reported. During the course of her hospitalization, she maintained remarkable control through a rather harrowing course of treatment. Only once did she appear really shaken; her careful financial planning was possibly proving to be inadequate.

> The doctor told me my Blue Cross and Blue Shield would cover the cost of the hospital, and treatments would be about another $250. But my Blue Cross is only for twenty-one days, and I am twenty-three days now, with over two weeks to go. The treatments will be $400. It is terrible. . . . You work hard all your life and get your home, and then they try to take it away from you. When I came here, they asked me all sorts of questions about insurance. Did we own our own home? How much money did we have in the bank? . . . Yes, I've seen it happen.

There were of course many values operative here, including the materialism of our culture, no doubt. Yet possibly the greatest threat to her was that she would be proved incompetent, that she would not live up to her own ideals. Here, as with the negative conscience, anger and the search for a scapegoat is one response to the threat. But unlike the values of the negative conscience, there was never any doubt in her mind that strength and ability were qualities she unambiguously wanted to possess. In anticipation, let it be noted that, while these were values in her positive conscience, they were still exercising their own kind of tyranny.

Guilt and Aspiration

Increasingly some writers of psychoanalytic theory have come to distinguish between guilt and shame, recognizing therein distinctly different types of moral dynamics. I suggest that as developed by them, this differentiation points to the contrasting motivations arising from the activity of the positive and negative consciences. None of these authors makes the distinction exactly as I have sought to do, but the cumulative effect of their work clearly lies in that direction.

Perhaps the earliest writer to raise this issue was Franz Alexander, although his terminology was not identical with ours. In 1938 he wrote a paper, "Remarks about the Relation of Inferiority Feelings and Guilt Feelings," associating the former with the "psychology of narcissism" and the latter with the "psychology of conscience." Unlike the dynamics of guilt, according to this article, inferiority feelings have a stimulating rather than an inhibiting effect on activity. "The feeling is not so much not being good in a moral sense but being weak, inefficient, unable to accomplish something. In inferiority feelings it is not implied, as it is in guilt feelings, that the self-condemnation is the result of wrong-doing."[14] Inferiority feelings are the result of failure, not transgression. They are an expression of self-rejection rather than the fear of rejection by another, even an internalized other. One may recall, in this context, our example of the woman suffering under the tyranny of her positive conscience. In contrast, Alexander gives the term "guilt" the traditional Freudian connotation. "One feels guilt because one wants to attack or has attacked somebody who does not deserve it. Such a sense of justice must be present if we are to speak of genuine guilt feelings because whenever one feels that a hostile intention or attack is justified, guilt feelings disappear."[15] Here he has introduced the positive, emotional content that changes fear to guilt. One has violated standards which are honored; one has attacked a neighbor who deserves a more loving response.

With Erik Erikson, we have the adoption of the same terminology used in our discussion. He differentiates between the dynamics of guilt and shame in his scheme for the eight stages of ego development, presenting a picture in harmony with Alexander's, although differing in emphasis because of his great interest in the role of culture and society. Shame is seen as self-consciousness, an awareness that one is inadequate and laid open to public view, a "sense of having exposed himself prematurely and foolishly."[16] To be more accurate, this is the nature of the child's early experience, an experience which—like social anxiety and guilt before the parents—is later internalized, resulting in the intrapsychic sense of shame, of being exposed before one's ego ideal. Shame involves anger, but it is one's own anger against himself and not that of another. Erikson's major contribution to the discussion of guilt is detailing its psychosocial development, in contrast to the classical Freudian psychosexual emphasis. Like Freud, however, he associates guilt with the fear of retaliation and thus with inhibition. Paul Pruyser has summarized Erikson's position as follows: "Guilt promotes conformity to moral standards by submission and renunciation; shame promotes conformity by identification with standards and by aspiration to them as ideals and values."[17]

Both Alexander and Erikson place the foundation of the dynamics of shame prior to those of guilt, in what Alexander calls the "pre-social" period. For Erikson the patterns of shame originate in what is analogous to the anal stage, guilt arising thereafter with the onset of the phallic period. This is precisely what one should expect if shame is associated with the introjection of the child's first and essentially unambivalent relation to parental figures, whereas guilt represents the internalization of parental restrictions arising from such relationships as they become marked by ambivalence.

These authors, and one could add others such as Piers and Singer,[18] agree in correlating shame with self-esteem, with goals, with desired values; and guilt with the internalized fear of the other, with social restriction, with values to which only ambivalent allegiance is given. Conceding their distinction between true moral desire and ethical restraint, in each case they define the ethical motivation negatively as guilt and shame. Here I would make one further observation. The primary connotation of guilt is fear of retaliation and feelings of remorse following upon aggression against a loved object or value. Thus it is basically an emotion arising after transgression, a feeling experienced after the act. In a derivative sense, guilt may be experienced proleptically, in which case it functions as moral restraint. Acting in this latter sense, it is a negative, ethical motivation. Similarly, shame is the experience of self-rage and self-rejection stemming from one's failure to achieve a desired goal. It too is an emotion arising after the act. By analogy, one could argue that it would function as a negative ethical motivation when experienced in anticipation. Such an argument, however, would be in danger of overlooking the fact that shame itself is the negative correlate of a prior, positive emotion, the desire to achieve a value. I suggest, then, that our basic moral motivation would be better described as guilt and aspiration than as guilt and shame. Generally speaking, is it not more accurate to describe someone as governed by aspiration than driven by the threat of shame? This concentration upon the negative rather than the positive may be reflecting the same bias we have already observed in the psychoanalytic treatment of morality.

Shame and Inhibition

I have just maintained that there are two basic moral motivations (in the psychological sense): guilt and aspiration. The former is associated with inhibition, the latter with stimulation. I suggested, furthermore, that shame is the negative feeling aroused when one fails to reach those standards which are the focus of positive aspiration and that in a sense one could speak of the anticipation of shame as an incentive to strive for a goal, shame as a quickening factor. Without denying that this is the usual expression for the dynamics of shame, let us now examine the possibility that under certain conditions it may act as a source of inhibition rather than stimulation, functioning in a manner directly analogous to guilt. In so doing, we shall see again the potential for moral tyranny arising from the positive conscience.

An individual may strongly aspire to attain a goal which has been set unrealistically above his potential or which he believes is beyond his capacities. If convinced in advance that he will prove a failure, rather than actually strive and fail he may choose to make no effort, thereby leaving open the possibility that he could have succeeded. In such a situation shame becomes the basic motivation, and like guilt, the anticipated experience of shame functions as a negative, inhibiting force.

Miss A. was a fifty-four-year-old single woman of German parentage who came to North America just prior to World War II. She was admitted to the hospital with a skin condition which produced massive blisters on every part of her body. If unchecked, the disease would prove fatal. She had been in treatment for several months before being transferred to a ward under my care. By this time her blistering had been controlled through the administration of large doses of cortisone, but her skin was still discolored.

Miss A. would quickly impress one as a person who prided herself on being extremely capable in a wide range of fields. She had engaged extensively in athletics all her life and held medals won at track competitions in Germany. Originally, she had come to the United States to teach swimming and other athletics professionally. (I gathered that she had been sent away from home to make good on her own. "My father told me," she remarked, "to come over here and see what I could do.") Unable to locate a teaching position in athletics and caught in the United States at the outbreak of hostilities, Miss A. had been forced to seek other employment. Nonetheless, until the onset of her present illness, she had continued to be active in sports, taking part in skiing, water skiing, golf, and tennis. She kept a box of photographs of herself engaged in various sports, proudly showing me a picture of herself with her Irish setter. "I would hunt pheasants with him at 5:00 A.M. on weekends," she said.

Miss A.'s talents, as she described them, were not limited to athletics; she saw herself as one who was generally capable.

My brother used to say that I could always get what I wanted in life—like when my mother was sick. This was in '48. I could not get on a ship, so I went to see a big shot with one of the companies. He came from our town. I told him he would have to help me. He did. He got me on a freighter which carried arms, and I was the only passenger. When I tried to come back to America again, I couldn't get a booking, so I went to a man I didn't know and said that I must get a ship. He got me one. Father always said never to be afraid of anyone, and I wasn't. It didn't matter to me if they had a million or a penny. This same drive and efficiency had governed her new vocation. "You see the war came along just then.... So I was here, and I had to find new work. I turned to accounting and worked at it very hard. It has taken me years to work up to where I was. The competition is keen, and then there are lots of young people with college degrees coming out all the time. I worked hard to get where I was." Miss A. had apparently gone quite far in her new field.

This self-ideal of the competent, efficient woman, always in command of things, was precisely what had been devastated by her disease. Hers was now a dependent status which she found very hard to accept.

> I have so many friends. I worked hard to keep my friends. I have had them since I came to this country. When you have no family you must keep friends, but it requires work. Family must stay with you, but friends don't have to. I have good friends, and they all want to do things for me. I have to be careful what they do in case one does more than another.... They all want to give me things, but I find it so hard to accept.

Chaplain: You mean it is easier to give?

Patient: Yes. I have always given things to my friends, not big gifts but little things. I always felt, as long as I could give them things, that I was wealthier, I was better off. It is hard to receive when you have always given.

Chaplain: We all have to receive at times.

Patient: My friends tell me that it is about time I was sick, that I never had any problems. I never have been sick. I always felt that as long as I had my health I could handle things. But now I am sick. They say it is my turn. They are only joking, of course, but it is not a very good joke.

Miss A.'s humiliation stood between herself and her family. At one of our first meetings, the patient showed me a picture of her quite young looking, widowed mother, adding immediately,

> I could not go to her. I have no money; I need welfare. It would kill her to think that I was on welfare. We were a very proud family. She could not accept welfare. It is a disgrace to her.

Chaplain: And yourself?

Patient: [*She closed her eyes and nodded.*] I think it is a disgrace too.

Some weeks later, during the Christmas season, the patient turned again to this subject, in response to her receipt of mail from Germany.

Patient: They want me to come home when I get out of a convalescent home.

Chaplain: Will you go?

Patient: Oh, no. I could not go like this. I need to be taken care of.

Chaplain: Maybe they would like to take care of you.

Patient: Oh, yes, they would, but I don't want that. When I go home I shall go on my own steam.... Call it "pride," chaplain.... Besides, I have used up all my money. I could not even buy a ticket.

Chaplain: Perhaps they would send you the money.

Patient: They would, but I could not ask for it. I told you before that I always find it hard to take. I would rather give. I guess that is pride, too, but that is the way I am.

Thus far Miss A. impresses us as a woman who is governed—to a significant extent—by a very high, demanding ideal. In our terminology, she is possessed of a very strong and exacting positive conscience. Her self-esteem is bound up with her capacity to succeed, and she knows no peace with failure. She is therefore, at one level, stimulated by her shame to regain her position as a competent, efficient, and independent woman. This much would appear clear.

As suggested, though, an exalted and potent ideal may also be the source of inhibiting shame. My interpretation of Miss A.'s behavior is admittedly speculative, but I would venture to say that there are indications of this in her actions.

A major element in the contemporary expression of Miss A.'s demanding self-image involved her advancement in the accounting business. Practically her first words to me were about being sent out "on her own" to do a "big" job just before she had taken sick. (This theme frequently reappeared in her conversation.) Several weeks later, I asked about the effect of the disease on her plans.

Chaplain: What would you have liked to do, if you had not taken sick?

Patient: My work. I work for an accounting firm. I have been with this particular firm for fifteen years and had just received a promotion. My first job on my own, but I only worked two months before I got sick. I had no time to prove whether I could do the job or not. . . .

Chaplain: What do you miss most?

Patient: My work, of course. It was very interesting. But I have lost my big chance. When I am strong, I shall have to start again at a lower job. Maybe I'll have another chance some day. Right now I am concentrating on getting my health.

The patient made it very clear that she had not failed. "I had no time to prove whether I could do the job or not." She had lost this opportunity, but given another chance she might succeed. On other occasions, however, she asserted that her illness would forever deny her the chance to prove herself.

> I can't do my old job. I have bandages on my legs and a brace on my back which I must wear for two years. I can't get up and down like I used to do. People think that as an accountant you just sit at a desk all day, but I had sixty-two subsidiaries. I could not ask someone to bring me a book or a statement every time I needed one. But I liked that work, and the man I worked for liked my work. He told me, "I like you. You watch my nickels. Other people only watch dollars, but you watch my nickels. That way I make money." But I can't do that any more, so how can I get a job? I am too old and too sick to insure. The premiums will be so high that no one will hire me.

In effect she was saying, "I am forever barred from proving how successful I would have been."

Two additional facts must be presented. First of all, Miss A. repeatedly stressed that she was the innocent victim in this situation; doctors were to blame for all her troubles. In response to her remark that she had not had a chance to prove herself on the new job, I commented on her probable disappointment.

Chaplain: That was your biggest disappointment, then?

Patient: Oh, no. I just had a cold in February, and I went to the doctor. He gave me a pill which made me sick. Blue patches! So he gave me the antidote, and I broke out in blisters. It is disappointing to go to the doctor to get well only to be made sick. . . . I always used old grandma's remedies whenever I got sick. But other people told me

> to go to the doctor. I told him I didn't want to take any
> pills, but he said that they would not do me any harm. Go
> to the doctor to get well, and be made sick! When I came
> in here, there was nothing wrong with me but my skin.
> X-rays showed all my organs were good.... It all came
> from a pill and a series of things I picked up here.

The second fact to be noted concerns what the medical staff
described as the patient's refusal to cooperate in her healing.
Early in my time with Miss A., her nurse complained that the
patient was insisting she could not walk, even though she had
already done so briefly with the attendant. As the patient's health
improved (in the opinion of the doctors), steps were taken to
discharge her to a convalescent home, but she vigorously resisted
these efforts. She usually responded angrily to any suggestions
that she try harder to exercise and to regain her strength. In
short, Miss A. appeared reluctant to get well.

What is the role of inhibiting shame in this case? Obviously
Miss A. was strongly desirous of succeeding in her new accounting position. It is possible, however, that she was inwardly
dubious of her ability to handle the more demanding task. She
would therefore be inhibited by the anticipation of her shame; she
would wish to withdraw from a position in which her failure could
be revealed. Whether or not such psychological factors were
involved in the onset of her disease, one can surely speculate that
at least they operated to produce a secondary gain from her
illness. In the hospital it could never be proved that she was
incapable of fulfilling the new post, and it was not her fault that
she was in the hospital. Her continued "sickness" was partly a
consequence of the tyranny of her own ideals.

Conscious and Unconscious Morality

It is surely strange that the one whose genius disclosed the powerful workings of the unconscious and who taught mankind to
distinguish between unconscious and conscious dynamics, that
this man, Sigmund Freud, failed to give precise formulation to
the distinction between conscious and unconscious moral structures. To be sure, he recognized the existence of both and introduced the concept "superego" to cope with the problem of
unconscious guilt feelings. Unfortunately, however, he did not

develop any specific terminology by which his references to this subject could be made precise. Instead, he usually combined both conscious and unconscious factors under the general terms "morality," "conscience," or "superego."

Shortly after the publication of *The Ego and the Id*, Franz Alexander, recognizing the necessity for a clear differentiation between conscious and unconscious moral functioning, suggested that such a distinction might be developed from Freud's work. So it was that in *The Psychoanalysis of the Total Personality* he proposed that "the conscious conscience, the first result of identification with the introjected parents, should continue to be designated the *ego-ideal*, and that the term *super-ego* be reserved for the ego-ideal which has later become unconscious...."[19] While this definition again missed the fact of moral aspiration, Alexander at least set forth terminology which permits a clearer distinction between conscious and unconscious moral activity. It may well have been this unfortunate choice of terms, however, which caused him to miss the distinction between the ego ideal and superego which had been implied in his work on inferiority feelings.

Similarly, Rogers speaks of distortion in and denial of awareness finally giving way (through therapy) to the congruence of self and experience, to the acceptance of formerly denied dimensions of that self's experience such as hatred of one's parents. This terminology, I suggest, is equally inadequate to deal with the full scope of unconscious moral functioning, for it is possible to be guided significantly by intrapsychic moral structures of which we are unaware, structures which are nonetheless congruent with the standards and self-image of our conscious personality. The question of unconscious morality is not fully handled by invoking the concept of incongruence. More light may be thrown by discussing the relationship between the conscious and unconscious "moral" functions of the mind under the headings (1) pseudo morality and (2) automatization.

1. The existence of pseudomoral reactions has long been recognized. Freud does not use this term, but obviously, as he describes the role of the superego in the etiology of neurosis, he sees it as not moral in any true sense. Rather, it is an irrational activity, masquerading under the guise of morality.

Charles Odier has offered a relatively complete treatment of this subject in his book *Les deux sources consciente et inconsciente de la vie morale*, where, as the title suggests, his primary purpose is to study the interaction of conscious and unconscious morality. His discussion is particularly useful to us because he endeavors to recognize both the psychological and the ethical aspects of this problem. Odier depicts the superego as an autonomous system which interjects itself, as a consequence of repression, between the unconscious and the ego, between the repressed and the moral conscience. There it fulfills the role of intercessor between the unconscious drives and the values of the ego, employing the techniques of compromise. But often it succeeds in satisfying neither claim, merely leading to a state of unrest and to periodic upsurges of moral and religious neuroses.

Odier reveals to us that, while in content the superego may be regarded as a collection of diverse moral processes, these are moral only in form, not in fact. Early on he remarks that all motives issuing from the unconscious, including those of the superego, are directed to the satisfaction of needs—without regard to the social, moral, or spiritual consequences; they are amoral. Thus, while conceptualized in terms of moral categories, the functioning of the superego is really pseudomoral. "Unconscious morality," in this context, means neither that a person is unaware of moral ideas pertaining to his activity nor that he is unconscious when functioning morally. Rather, it implies that the true motives governing his behavior, i.e., the unconscious motives, are unknown and unknowable, and although they appear as moral through the masking action of the superego, they are in fact amoral. To insure clarity, Odier prefers the terms "superego activity" or "pseudo morality" rather than "unconscious morality." In short, "pseudo morality" draws attention to what is actually a nonmoral functioning of the superego. While often a matter of considerable therapeutic import, it is not per se a matter for ethical adjudication. (This is only one facet of the superego in Odier's understanding. The exposition of the other carries us into what is more properly a matter of "unconscious morality.")

2. Turning now to automatization, we become aware of a *salutary* superego.

When Alexander expounds his concept of the "corruptibility of the neurotic superego," he makes reference to "the gradual automatization of the conscience reaction."[20] For analogy, he refers to a child learning to avoid a burning candle; the child develops a conscious inhibition of the motor response and no longer reaches for the flame. Such inhibition corresponds to the conscious rejection, by the moral conscience, of some value or impulse. The inhibitory process may later become internalized, so that it functions automatically, even denying to the conscious ego any awareness of the impulse. Alexander comments that moral inhibition may be similarly internalized and function without the ego being aware of what has been rejected.

Such an unconscious, automatic functioning of repression has a twofold advantage over conscious moral control. The first is economic. Since instincts can be regulated to accord with social requirements without involving the conscious ego, the latter is thereby freed to engage in other essential activities. We need not decide anew each day against murder or incest but may turn our attention to reflecting upon new moral judgments. There is also an affective advantage wherein the ego is saved from the experience of anticipated guilt and from undergoing the conflict between temptation and guilt. Of course such advantages are not achieved without the loss of some contemporary discrimination; automatic functioning is cruder and more schematic than that of the conscious moral conscience. (We shall return to this problem in the final chapter.)

Still later, Alexander reverts to this subject, stressing that the recognition of moral automatisms implies not two sharply distinguished entities but, rather, a continuum. "Here again it is advisable to distinguish between more and less automatic emotional reactions and behaviour rather than between a completely automatic superego and a conscious, more flexible ego."[21]

In *Ego Psychology and the Problem of Adaptation*, Heinz Hartmann devotes a chapter to the development and significance of "preconscious automatisms." He tells us that, just as motor behavior becomes routinized and automatic, so may perception and thinking. He also recognizes a continuum between completely automatized and flexible behavior. Pathological automatisms (which correspond to the aforementioned neurotic, nonmoral superego) play a major role in some mental illnesses, but automatisms per se are not necessarily a pathological development. Hartmann stresses the functional value of automatic moral responses which are in accord with the basic values of one's culture. Such superego activity represents a salutary adaptation to society. (From an ethical viewpoint, of course, social adaptation is not necessarily beneficial, but adaptation to the real or idealized culture which embodies one's true values does have functional advantages.) Automatisms, Hartmann asserts, are in an ambiguous position relative to mental health, but they should not automatically be dismissed as pathological. "The normal ego must be *able* to control," he writes, "but it must also be *able to must*; and this fact, far from vitiating it, is necessary for its health."[22]

Odier's study throws additional light in this area. He alludes to a "normal" superego, by which he means the superego as it functions in the psychologically healthy person, in one who shows neither impulsive acting out nor neurotic conflict. Moreover, he differentiates between two functions within the superego, designating them "Bergsonian" and "Freudian."[23]

The Bergsonian function represents a precipitate from the general cultural evolution of mankind; it is a product of social history. "It is composed of processes of automatization designed to regulate the relationship of the individual with the group.... It saves the ego the obligation and difficulty of ceaselessly recommencing the same endeavor for adaptation and renunciation."[24] Odier points out that such an automatic, socialized superego naturally tends to be inflexible and routinized, which accounts for the occasional apparent irrationality of its activity. But this Bergsonian superego, he believes, is in quite close contact with the conscious ego: presumably it is the surface of the superego where contact has not yet been lost with the ego. The automatic responses of the social precipitate are open to a degree of recall and reevaluation by the moral conscience: we can still reconsider our social adaptation. But the automatization of our adaptation is normally a gain, both socially and psychologically.

The Freudian function within the superego arises from individual (as opposed to cultural) history or evolution and is charged with controlling the primitive, instinctual drives—specifically the aggressive, the masochistic, and the asocial, erotic impulses. As with the Bergsonian, the Freudian becomes gradually automatized, thereby playing a supportive role in the ego's moral development. This latter function is subject to the pathological distortion which leads to neurosis but in the normal personality is beneficial.

Odier would not have us visualize a sharp separation between the two superego functions. He reminds his readers that the Bergsonian superego, derived basically from the collective, still shows individual modifications in any given person and consequently carries Freudian characteristics as well. I personally would suggest that the strictly Bergsonian function is also open to pathological distortion which can express itself in mass neurosis, in the pathological religious expressions assailed by Freud. One might well speculate upon the operation of a pathological Bergsonian superego, for example, in the rise of Nazism.

The successive application of the distinction between conscious and unconscious and between the positive and negative consciences produces a fourfold division within the conscience, one which Odier has recognized by naming each structure. The unconscious and largely automatic moral functions he calls the superego and the ego ideal, the primitive negative and positive consciences. Then, with the advent of maturity, the superego is increasingly replaced—in a situation of mental health—by the "moral conscience," while the role of the ego ideal is assumed more and more by conscious "personal ideals."

5   Moral Confrontation in Therapy

We have now sufficient data to address more adequately the central problem faced in this book. In fact the split between psychology and ethics, as we have seen, raises two separate but related topics. As noted, the reluctance to issue a moral challenge in therapy reflects in part a growing disillusionment in modern society with all authority, as well as the insertion of a covert morality under the guise of psychologically founded fact. But I have argued that human existence always has a moral dimension, a reality only made more urgent by the significant ethical aspects in the major social crises of our time. Any therapy, therefore, which seeks on these or any other grounds to avoid a true ethical witness is bound to be inadequate because of its failure to equip counselees to function in the real world, a world of moral choices. Moral confrontation in therapy is thus an ethical necessity. We are now in a position, however, to clarify its purely therapeutic function as well. This, then, is the first issue and will be the focus of the present chapter, the ethical and therapeutic functions of moral confrontation. But in Chapter 1 we saw that a more significant reason for the avoidance of moral confrontation is associated with the problem of moralism, with the seemingly inevitable clash between presenting a moral demand and offering the unconditional acceptance essential to therapeutic progress. (Behavior modification was the exception to this rule, since it engages rather freely in making moral and quasi-moral demands.) This constitutes our second basic issue. Is all morality necessarily moralistic, or can we establish the possibility of a nonmoralistic morality? The full explication of this issue requires a further engagement between theology and psychology and will be the topic of my final chapter.

Although I have not emphasized the distinction between fear and guilt up to this point, let me briefly draw attention to its implications before exploring the therapeutic function of moral confrontation. Society may define a particular standard as a moral value, but it only becomes such for the individual *psychologically* when his relation to it is characterized by positive emotions, ambivalent or otherwise. Where there is no substratum of love or respect, behavior is governed by amoral fear. Love is the structural foundation of the individual's recognition of a moral value. Gotthard Booth has expressed this idea by distinguishing between authority as the *power* and as the *right* to command. A truly *moral* authority is one possessing the *right* to command obedience. In this connection, he asserts that "all authority is rooted in love."[1] He feels that the negative emphasis of Freudian theory has often tended to obscure this primary fact. René Spitz's work with hospitalized and foundling home children and Lauretta Bender's on the problem of psychopathic behavior in the young provide clinical support for the importance of love in the formation of "psychologically moral" values.[2] They assert that the absence of a basic loving and trusting relationship with significant others in childhood encourages a vote against emotional membership in the human race, if not through the infant's withdrawal into mental retardation, then through the delinquent's refusal to give allegiance to the moral values of his community. This has obvious implications for the counselor who would assist in creating both moral and mental health.

Moral Witness in the Context of Counseling

As I have said, the understanding of conscience outlined in this work makes clear the fact that the issue of moral values cannot be excluded from the therapeutic domain. Mental health is to be achieved not simply on the analyst's couch or in the supportive group therapy session but, of necessity, in a real world where moral decisions must be made. Even to decide to enter therapy to relieve some vague and debilitating sense of anxiety, when one could have opted to bear his own disquiet and engage in a civil rights protest, is to make both a moral and a psychological choice. To be whole in a world where racial prejudice, economic injustice, political oppression, and a host of domestic vices infect the lives of men and women inevitably requires that one confront the ethical realm for both psychotherapeutic and social reasons. To ignore this confrontation would be not only to fail morally but to lapse into a new form of mental illness, to be accommodated to an unreal world, an amoral, crisis-less global T-group in which nothing has abiding ethical significance. (It was precisely at this point, with their different evaluation of the natural moral inclina-

tions of the human race, that Freud and Rogers parted company.)
The ethical realities of our current human situation—was it ever
otherwise?—make the moral imperative an essential dimension
of personal healing.

*   *   *

At the very time I was writing this section, I happened to
be doing some reading in the area of marriage enrichment,
small-group programs to assist couples in essentially good marriage relationships with a view to making them even better. By
chance the mailman brought my monthly copy of the *New Inter-
nationalist*, a magazine sponsored by a group of Christian organi-
zations concerned with the problems of poverty, ecology, and the
needs of the Third World. I immediately sensed in myself the old
tension. Why should I spend my time helping middle-class white
couples in the affluent West to get more enjoyment and fulfillment out of their marriages when the only thing so many couples
in the rest of the world would seek is the joy of seeing their
children get enough to eat? Is the whole counseling process the
application of a Band-Aid, when the festering sore requires radical surgery? To feel such uneasiness is, I suspect, an inevitable
uneasiness that comes with the burden of awareness.

If I may bear witness to some of my own value judgments,
the counselor who never knows such tension is not present to his
client as a full human being. Nevertheless, to heal, to enrich an
individual human life, whether or not one thereby improves the
larger social context, is a humanly meaningful goal. Why otherwise would one ever seek to support the dying with counseling?
How pathetic if we were ever to find ourselves in the morally odd
position of helping someone in the Third World not because of
the intrinsic worth of that individual but because his improvement would aid some larger abstraction called "society"! I suspect, further, that the man or woman who has found inner peace
and wholeness, while not automatically more loving, is probably
more open to face the moral and social responsibilities of world
citizenship. So my tension remains, but it can be a creative
tension. It spurs me on both in counseling and in working as best
I can for a just social order in my country and throughout the
world. In all likelihood it will be the free, whole, and psychologi-

cally sound members of our affluent West who will be ready first to make the sacrifices necessary to foster this end.

*   *   *

To continue our main discussion, social ethics aside, therapeutic realities of counseling require a clarification of and a confrontation with the whole realm of moral values. Even in a world devoid of the socioethical crises that mark our times, the therapist would need to face with his patient the question of the latter's—and as we shall see, the counselor's own—moral values. Let me suggest several factors here.

1. *Unconscious morality.*—Conscience, as we have seen, has both conscious and unconcious elements, the latter taking the form of more or less automatic reactions, and this has major implications for the counselor and for therapy. Moral automatization can play a useful role in conscience functioning to the extent that it is adapted to the realities of the environment and to one's conscious ideal.

Two forms of maladaptation are distinguishable, however. Odier directs our attention to one, *pseudo morality*. Here instinctual patterns become intellectualized in terms of moral categories; unconscious need satisfactions masquerade as ethical values. What is required is a clarification of the true motivations governing behavior. A classical example would be Freud's anal personality, whose great emphasis upon cleanliness and order is an unconscious reaction formation against his preoccupation with the bowel function. Perhaps a less extreme example would be more helpful for those not baptized in the Freudian faith. A mother exhibits an excessively protective concern for her child; this is a major demand of her maternal conscience. He must not climb trees lest he fall and break a bone. He must not ride his bike on the road lest he be struck by a car. He must not play in the mud for fear of germs. In actuality, the mother may be governed by a deep-seated hostility toward her child and her maternal role and, under the guise of concern for the youngster, may unconsciously be exercising a cruel tyranny over him. In such cases, therapy can only proceed through a direct encounter with the "values" in question.

Another form of disruptive automatization is one we might well call *moral maladaptation*. Here the child's simplified framework for moral reference continues to function automatically in the adult, limiting the latter's ability to make adequate discriminations. Many forms of prejudice are examples of such ethical pathology. For the child, the "good" is that which gains parental approval and "evil" that which they abhor. As such it does not represent moral discrimination by the child. If parents fear, distrust, or despise others because of the color of their skin or their place of worship, the child can easily adopt these categorical reactions, growing up to reject such "outsiders." His prejudice will undoubtedly be reinforced by the in-group's rationale for superiority, but its greatest strength will lie in his deep, unconscious, childhood judgment of value, a judgment untested by the realities of his adult circumstances and experiences. Healing requires a reexamination of these moral presuppositions.

Sometimes, for example, it is hard for us who stand outside the situation to comprehend how the white minorities of southern Africa can close their eyes to the political, social, and economic realities of their situation, to the inevitable surge for freedom among the black population of their homelands, especially given the experience of so many newly liberated nations on that continent. Even if they are not stirred by the moral issues of justice and human dignity, how can all these other instances be ignored! Here on a cultural scale is the power of moral maladaptation: so deeply a part of their identity are these assumptions of racial superiority and fear of blacks! Yet these attitudes were learned not from grossly evil people but from parents who loved and cared for them as children, from friends and relatives who were kind, cultured, and educated and who taught them much concerning life in those early years. It is indeed a major task to raise these assumptions to the light of reconsideration, and for many it may ultimately be the collapse of the society which forces their reexamination. But for some it can also be a healing encounter.

Finally, the presence of moral automatisms (as part of the individual sense of identity) is relevant to the relationship between law and contextual decision. These, I suggest, provide a set or bias which will influence all ethical choices. A moral decision represents a response of the whole person in context, not just an isolated judgment made on the basis of some rule of conduct.

(Theologically, one may wish to interpret this type of response as an immediate encounter with the divine command as opposed to law.) But let us not forget that the individual's identity is a critical part of the context, that his moral automatisms are significant determinants of all decisions. He is never simply a naked ego. Consequently the laws which have been laid down in his conscious and unconscious sense of identity will, in large measure, direct his conduct. The issue for the counselor is whether such laws result in a morally viable identity. Brunner would allow that law, in the form of an external code, is relevant prior to decision; as a source of guidance, it is part of the context within which decision is made. Now we see its relevance even prior to the context of decision, for the external codes accepted in the past continue in the present identity, in the moral automatisms which characterize every human being.

Alexander maintains that automatization is a process. He further remarks that we should picture a continuum of more or less automatic forms of behavior rather than a sharp dichotomy between a fully automatized superego and a flexible ego. Hence we may say that the incorporation of moral values involves not only the acceptance of standards as personally authoritative but also the gradual automatization of their functioning in ethical decisions. This becomes particularly important for those counselors who, by virtue of their role, stand openly in some ethical tradition. The pastoral task in Christian education or catechetics, for instance, is to present a system of values which will be conducive to a Christlike identity. But the counselor's assignment always arises in relation to the established identity of his client. He may need to assist the latter in reversing the process of incorporation and in reestablishing conscious discrimination over some moral automatisms, that these may be modified and lead to an identity in keeping with his and his community's highest ideals. Assuredly this is more properly the role of the moral guide than the secular counselor. Yet even the latter may for therapeutic reasons need to reverse the process of automatization where such functioning leads to internal conflict.

2. *The moral rebuke in therapy.*—The therapist is not the only one to question the value of good conduct achieved by a moral rebuke. As a theologian, C. Ellis Nelson strongly criticizes

such conduct, describing it as sub-Christian. He feels that the Christian education of conscience must lead us beyond the inhibiting negative conscience to the aspiring positive one.[3] Each of the theologians studied in developing our theological understanding of conscience would surely agree that morality based on the first use of the law is a less than fully Christian response. Such obedience is dictated by self-interest rather than love for God and one's neighbor. Yet they would acknowledge that the negative conscience plays a valid role in the life of man as an instrument of divine activity. Similarly, I suggest, the negative conscience, when experienced as a moral rebuke, has a valid role within the counseling relationship—a role which must not be ignored merely because it is regarded as "sub-Christian." Actually it is a role recognized explicitly in behavior modification and implicitly in Freud.

Theologically speaking, one function of the negative conscience is to act as a restraint upon sinful man and thereby preserve some degree of social order and justice. Here the religionist finds an ally in Freud, despite his criticism of conventional morality. E. Frederick Proelss—quite naturally as a prison chaplain—places considerable value upon the negative conscience in curbing what he regards as our sociopathic instincts.[4]

The Reformers said that law in its first use, bridling the wicked, was a necessary social condition for the preaching of the gospel. For their part, therapists—Rogerians included, I suspect—must acknowledge that in some instances a categorical imperative, even a moral imperative, may be needed to curb the patient in order to provide the minimal conditions for therapy. The violent and angry client may only be brought to the point where therapy can begin by encountering a law which declares that violence will be met with strict punishment. (The administration of electroshock treatments or drugs is in this sense akin to an imposition of law—perhaps peace purchased through punishment.) Quite apart from such extreme examples, behavior modification operates on the explicit assumption that healing purely docile patients also depends upon the judicious use of rewards and punishments. While behavior modification per se does not offer an interpretive scheme which can deal with moralism—moralism is an inner state and thus unconceptualized in such theory—nevertheless, we have already stressed that it must be seen as a moralistic mode of reformation. It is perhaps sub-Christian or, rather, does not achieve full moral maturity. Indeed the moral meaning of behavior to the patient is not really faced at all. Still, in some cases at least, it does achieve transformations which are both individually and socially beneficial. If this is true, the counselor cannot afford to rule out categorically a moral rebuke as part of the "therapeutic" encounter. (We have yet, of course, to meet the issue of moralism per se.)

An inevitable tension remains for those who accept the validity of a moral reprimand. Even if his patient is well adjusted and content, the counselor may need to confront him if that happy life-style is immoral. The child raised in a sociopathic subculture, in a Bonnie-and-Clyde type of family, needs major moral reeducation, a task requiring significant counseling skills. Yet the counselor faces a dilemma. Dare he be content simply to accept the moral definitions of society? Is his task merely to insure conformity thereto? The conduct of therapy, and especially the invocation of a moral reproof, inevitably forces one to struggle with the larger issues of the meaning of humanness and the qualities of a truly human life, with the definitions of health and salvation.

Our theological description affirms another value of law in its first use when it is acting as a preliminary discipline for those who will ultimately be converted. Allied to this is law in its second use, which leads to an intensified experience of the negative conscience and can thus be instrumental in preparing the way for the acceptance of divine grace. To be sure, these are issues which arise only for those engaged self-consciously in the pastoral task. They do, however, add another reason for the pastoral counselor to consider the careful witness of a moral censure.

Time and again it has been urged in this study that the counselor bear witness to the ethical imperatives of life, but he cannot be certain that the client's acceptance of such values—if accepted at all—will be wholehearted, that they will form part of his positive conscience. Still, their incorporation into the negative conscience may be a valuable first step in the development of moral health. While the positive conscience remains his ideal, the counselor can acknowledge and respect the role of the negative conscience, serving to benefit, as it does, both the client and society.

3. *Guilt versus aspiration: a further complexity.*—Much psychotherapy in the past has emphasized the negative conscience, tending to assume automatically that the counselor's task is to help the client overcome the repressive activity of a severe conscience, to aid him in expressing feelings which he has been withholding. This viewpoint underlies the free-expression emphasis in some child-training programs and continues to guide some psychotherapists and pastoral counselors. The unquestioned acceptance of this position is challenged, however, by the recognition of the distinctly different dynamics operative in the positive and negative consciences. It runs the risk of confusing aspiration and guilt.

Gerhart Piers cites the therapeutic liabilities which may result from such a confusion. He refers, for example, to the efforts of a therapist to get someone "to experience and express his hostilities."[5] Insofar as the patient's difficulty is a consequence of guilt-repressed aggressiveness (that is, insofar as such repression is excessive and not fully understood by the patient), such encouragement, rather than liberating, will only intensify his experience of shame because of his failure to be aggressive. Let me add another possibility. If nonaggressiveness or gentleness is a strong value of his positive conscience, then such calls for increased militancy may actually be an attack on the basis of his self-esteem.

Consider again the patient who expressed so much anger over the injustices of life: his own illness and the sentence given those who had robbed his father-in-law's store. Despite the inequities, however, he would not change; he would stay good. What would be the effect of telling him to ease off on his conscience and to start living it up when released from hospital? If he suffers solely from the tyranny of an overly strict negative conscience, such advice could be experienced as liberating. But there are other possibilities. Even assuming that his value constellation lies entirely in the negative conscience, then challenging his moral standards might only undermine a shaky security. Though he may have transgressed the moral law, at least he has not committed robbery or cheated on his wife. But now the counselor questions the significance of this virtue. If, on the other hand, part of his righteousness represents values of the positive conscience, to urge a morally relaxed mode of existence would be to suggest that his life goals were of little importance. Neither of these latter approaches is apt to be therapeutic.

There is yet another danger in the immediate assumption that a given value forms part of the repressive negative conscience. By encouraging freer self-expression, the counselor may actually be fostering the acceptance of values he himself would repudiate. Take the example of hostility. By encouraging the client to express his hostility, the therapist may seem to imply that aggressiveness and hostility should be valued in the positive conscience, that self-assertion is at all times a prized moral attribute.

What stance, then, should we as counselors take in response to what we consider the extreme or unhealthy values proclaimed by the counselee? Any direct attempt to alter such an ethical commitment can founder unless we ascertain whether such values are part of the positive or negative conscience, or possibly a mixture. But frequently such insight is not readily available. A pastor, for example, unless he chooses to embark on a long depth relationship with his parishioner, will normally be required to take some concrete action before he has discerned the counselee's relation to the values involved. His action therefore must be one which is potentially therapeutic in every eventuality.

In general, our counseling task is twofold: to aid the client in gaining sufficient liberty to reexamine his ethical commitment and to bear witness to our own ethical position. In theological terms, failure to do the second openly amounts to preaching a truncated gospel of the love of God which ignores His holiness and, as we have just seen, may actually have a disruptive effect on the counseling process. A primary requirement for effective counseling, I contend, is honesty, more exactly a dual honesty.

Rieff has described Freud's therapy as encouraging an "ethic of honesty," for the patient is thereby encouraged to become knowledgeable about the values which actually govern his behavior. The primary requirement is that he recognize his true feelings and commitments and face up to their consequences. This is a goal which the counselor must adopt for his client. But left with this alone, we have what can equally be called an empty ethic. Honesty is also required on the part of the counselor. He must faithfully bear witness to his own moral values. Thus, while encouraging a counselee to be honest concerning his feelings of hostility, the pastor (say) must be honest in revealing to him his own understanding of the place of hostility and aggressiveness in the Christian life. The timing and mode of his ethical pronouncements are of course critical. One can bear witness to the moral law in a manner which only intensifies the anguish of an already shattered conscience, seeming to deny the hope of grace and a new beginning. Yet alternatively, the casual dismissal or neglect of this dimension can be destructive of ethical and psychological health. The counselor who easily proclaims that adultery is really not so terrible, aside from the ethical adequacy or inadequacy of such a statement, may actually be dissipating the creative anxiety of an aroused negative conscience or shattering the self-respect of one whose only basis of hope is that he has been chaste. He may, in short, be hindering rather than advancing therapy. Obviously, an honest yet sensitive confrontation with the counselor's true convictions must occur for both moral and therapeutic reasons. Moreover, only thus does the client encounter one who will himself risk being rejected in an open confession of his own moral values, one who has experienced his right to be as grounded beyond the momentary responses of other men. Here, however, we are moving ahead of ourselves to the realm of the transmoral conscience.

In summary, we have seen that, not only for social and ethical reasons but for a variety of therapeutic reasons as well, the question of moral values cannot safely be avoided in counseling. Moreover, this ethical dimension cannot rest simply with the disinterested clarification of the client's values—though this is an important element therein—but must eventuate, on occasion, in a direct and honest confrontation with the moral values of the counselor, even with the possibility of a moral rebuke.

Let me hasten to add that a therapeutically effective and ethically responsible moral witness does not always require a moral rebuke. In many situations, quite the contrary. It may be far more effective to affirm the ethical virtues of the client, to build on his strength. Rather than fault another for being insensitive to the plight of the poor or for measuring a man's worth by his annual dollar income, greater moral transformation may be achieved by honest praise of the sincere empathy and compassion he shows for the handicapped or by commending the profound love and loyalty he exhibits toward friends. In so doing, we bear witness to important elements of the moral realities in the other person and also invite the establishment of a loving relationship with him which, as seen in Spitz and Bender, is the foundation of true morality. Yet sadly enough, all too often we are as reluctant to affirm another, to praise, to express affection, as we are to confront, rebuke, or express anger. Perhaps we are afraid to be truly honest in the expression of positive feelings, lest these be rejected and we ourselves feel threatened.

Nevertheless, we cannot simply rest our moral witness in all cases on affirmation alone lest, like the old lady who was consulted about Satan, we cite no moral failure but are content to praise his industry. The power and place of affirmation does not preclude the role of the ethical rebuke. Thus we are brought again to the basic issue behind this study, the problem of moralism. Can we so confront yet not be moralistic?

6   The Psychodynamics of
       a Nonmoralistic Morality

The distinction between the positive and negative consciences would indicate at least the possibility of a nonmoralistic morality.

Whenever ethical conduct is governed by values comprising a negative conscience, values functioning as law in its first use, the associated morality will inevitably take on a moralistic tone. Obedience is regarded as a prerequisite for the maintenance of some desired relationship. The child, in classical Freudian theory, obeyed his father in order to keep his love and to avoid physical punishment. The Rogerian child "learned" from his mother certain "conditions of worth" which he must meet to be acceptable. The sinner, living under law in its first use, submitted to the will of God in order to maintain a modicum of divine favor, the avoidance of divine wrath. Even the apparent compliance of the righteous could be motivated by a desire to earn eternal life. While such morality may serve a useful function both ethically and therapeutically, insofar as the values governing conduct are *imposed* from without and do not represent the individual's sincere *aspirations*, the accompanying morality will constitute a tyranny and the corresponding relationship will be moralistic. More precisely, although love may be present in the relationship, the latter will be determined by achievement.

The concepts of the positive conscience and the third use of the law, however, indicate a second possible relation to moral values which is not intrinsically moralistic. Obedience now represents a spontaneous expression of individual desires. Submission to the imposed will of the other is replaced by sincere aspiration to achieve those values or qualities observed in the other. The way is thus opened for a nonmoralistic relationship, one founded upon love rather than accomplishment.

Self-imposed Moralism: The Tyranny of Our Own Ideals
The possibility of a nonmoralistic morality has been suggested, but let us remember that the mere predominance of the positive conscience does not necessarily prevent the rise of moralism. One can impose upon himself a tyranny far worse than that inflicted

by another. The individual himself may rigorously demand achievement as the price of his right to be. Consequently, even if the counselor governs his behavior toward the client by the sincere belief that their relationship must be founded upon love or acceptance and not upon achievement, this does not preclude the client's incorporation of the values proclaimed into a moralistic ethic. Moralism is ultimately a manifestation of human sin. It may represent the sin of the counselor, who, through the pretense of morality, would exert an unwarranted authority over the client; or it may equally well attest to the latter's sin, for man in his pride does not readily accept the right to be as a gift, preferring to earn it.

Here let us note a danger peculiar to the counselor. He must be able to accept the possibility that the client will remain unwell, that the parishioner will continue to sin. If the therapist's self-esteem depends upon being successful in the relationship, then he will be operating under his own moral tyranny and will be more apt to evoke an answering moralism in the other. This does not mean that he should be indifferent or apathetic concerning the results of his therapeutic efforts. But he needs to strive for ever more effective modes of counseling while remaining free from the requirement to succeed. In this he must struggle with what Reinhold Niebuhr once called the "creative and destructive elements in anxiety."[1] He must resist the temptation for a moralistic witness, born of his need to justify himself through his success.

At the risk of overemphasis, let me illustrate yet again the dreadful tyranny of one's own ideals in what I choose to call a "value impasse." Here two or more conflicting values lie at the heart of the reaction, values invoked concurrently, resulting in a deadlock. The simultaneous application of guilt and aspiration, or of conflicting aspirations, renders all action useless. In this situation at least one of the conflicting values must represent the positive conscience, for an element of wholehearted desire is necessary to prevent the individual's complete withdrawal from the situation. This pattern is conspicuous in the case of some patients hospitalized for ulcers. It would seem that they turn their frustration against their own bodies.

Mrs. B. was a thirty-nine-year-old divorcee, the mother of

two young children and an advertising executive for a manu-facturing company. To the patient, her occupation represented many positive values. She strongly identified with her father and with the masculine role in general; she disliked women's groups. She enjoyed the aggressive nature of her position and the power it gave her. In addition, the financial rewards of an executive were appealing. "Money isn't everything, that is true, but you have to have money. I couldn't get near my salary in any other line. I suppose I could make it in the garment district if I worked like mad, but there isn't the security there. I am the only woman in seven thousand employees who is on the executive payroll. If I were a man I would get more, but I still do all right." My visit was interrupted by a telephone call from Mrs. B.'s secretary. The patient gave orders for spending large sums of money. Afterward she smilingly remarked, "You would think I was indispensable to the company—the way my phone is always ringing."

Coupled with her *vocational aspirations*, Mrs. B. dis-played a vigorous *ethical concern*. On a trip to the Middle East she had been denied admission to Jordan because her maiden name was mistakenly assumed to be Jewish. A consular official suggested that if she lost her passport he could issue another in her married name, but she refused. That would be dishonest! "If you cheat on such a thing, where do you stop?" she asked. This facet of her personality was clashing with her vocation.

Chaplain: Do you like your work?
Patient: A great deal of it.
Chaplain: You sound like you have some reservations.
Patient: Oh, I do. There is a lot of dirty work goes on in the fashion industry. It is not the glamorous field you might think from the outside. I don't like that aspect of it.
Chaplain: What do you mean exactly?
Patient: Well, we sell to the mills which make gray goods, the plain gray cloth woven from our fibers; these people sell to the printers who in turn sell to the clothing manu-facturers. Our company helps each of these with advertis-ing, but each is cutthroat and out to get all they can, not caring who gets hurt. I tell you, when I get home from work at night, I just want to take a shower to wash it off me. I just loathe that aspect of it all.

The patient later revealed that her father had been an advertising executive but had had to quit because he could not stand the immoral business practices which he encountered.

Mrs. B.'s impasse was quite clear. Her role as an executive was very important for her self-esteem, being a position of power (i.e., in her eyes masculine?) and similar to one held by her father, who was undoubtedly her hero. Yet this role forced her into association with business practices abhorrent to her strong moral convictions—convictions also derived from her father. Yet to this point, at any rate, the pull of the job was too strong to allow her to opt out as he had done. If her "ethical" concern was an element of her positive conscience, her value impasse arose from conflicting aspirations. If on the other hand it formed part of the negative conscience, something she must do to earn her father's respect, then she was caught between conflicting guilt and aspiration. In either case she was suffering partly because of the high demands of her own ideals (her vocational aspirations), regardless of whether her values were ethically sound.

Once more the importance of honesty: let us forget momentarily the soundness of her standards. Had I encouraged Mrs. B. not to feel guilty on the grounds that her role was simply part of the tough business world, then providing that she had been afflicted by pressures from the negative conscience, she might have felt truly liberated. If, however, her strong moral convictions were another aspect of her father that she wholeheartedly admired, such counsel could have been experienced as an assault upon her father and her own self-esteem.

Moralism and the Transmoral Conscience
While we anticipate the possibility of nonmoralistic morality and thus of nonmoralistic counseling, we have not dealt with this problem of self-imposed moralism; so far we have not coped with the tyranny of the positive conscience. To make the necessary modifications in our understanding of the conscience, and thereby of counseling, let us return to the theologians cited in the second chapter.

May I remind the reader of the method which has been evolving in this study? The theologian and the therapist as pure types seek different goals and attempt to conceptualize different dimensions of the moral life. The former would clarify our understanding of the *moral purpose* in the human experience of an ethical imperative, the latter the *psychodynamics* of the same reality. Furthermore, the pastor or therapist, as human being, will on occasion transcend his own role as expert and mediate the health or salvation which is the proper function of the other as expert. Insofar as his conceptualizations result from human as well as pastoral or therapeutic experience, they usually carry implicit insights into the other's realm of expertise. For example, the theological doctrine of the Three Uses of the Law assumes—at times fairly explicitly—a psychology of conscience quite in harmony with that of Freud and Rogers. In an analogous fashion, I propose therefore to set forth certain theological understandings by which the Reformers sought to meet the problem of moralism (or, as they called it, the tyranny of the Law) without thereby losing all sense of ethical urgency. Afterward we shall select the psychodynamic insights therein which enable the therapist to move beyond moralism to a transmoral conscience.

The parallels between justification by faith and therapeutic acceptance, with which we shall begin, have often been cited. We shall go beyond this, however, to explore the psychological implications of the Reformers' understanding of sanctification and its relationship to faith.

Justification by faith.—Paul Tillich has coined the term "transmoral conscience" to describe that quality of conscience which liberates the possessor from the tyranny of his own ideals: "A conscience may be called 'transmoral' which judges not in obedience to a moral law but according to the participation in a reality which transcends the sphere of moral commands. A transmoral conscience does not deny the moral realm, but it is driven beyond it by the unbearable tensions of the sphere of the law."[2] He adds, "Indeed, it is impossible *not* to transcend the moral conscience because it is impossible to unite a *sensitive* and a *good* conscience."[3] The transmoral conscience is therefore one which seeks to establish the individual's right to be as prior to any moral achievement. Tillich points out that Luther (and, we may also add, Calvin) proclaimed such a conscience in the doctrine of Justification by Grace through Faith.

This doctrine, usually abbreviated to Justification by Faith, has been given such emphasis in Reformation studies that it hardly seems necessary at this point to support Tillich's contention. However, let us cite the works of Luther, Calvin, and Brunner to illustrate the close connection between their understanding of this doctrine and their conception of the three uses of the law, thus making clear the application of "Justification by Faith" to the issue of a moralistic conscience.

Luther, we have seen, tends to use the term "law" as a correlate of "active" righteousness, that righteousness which man seeks to obtain by the merit of his own efforts; this he repudiates both as an impossibility and as an offense against the love and glory of God. Over against this he sets true Christian righteousness, which is by nature "passive." It is a gift; our justification is by grace. So he writes,

> Wherefore the afflicted and troubled conscience hath no remedy against desperation and eternal death, unless it take hold of the promise of grace freely offered in Christ, that is to say, this passive righteousness of faith, or Christian righteousness.... Thus I abandon myself from all active righteousness, both of mine own and of God's law, and embrace only that passive righteousness, which is the righteousness of grace, mercy and forgiveness of sins.[4]

Or still later,

> I speak not this to the end that the law should be despised, neither doth Paul so mean, but it ought to be had in great estimation. But because Paul is here in the matter of justification, it was necessary that he should speak of the law, as of a thing very contemptible and odious. For justification is a far other manner of thing than the law is.... When the conscience therefore is in conflict, then should it think upon nothing, know nothing at all but Christ only and alone.[5]

For Luther, the justice of God carries one beyond the valid claim of Divine Law to the exhilarating experience of His saving mercy. "I began to understand the Justice of God," he recalls, "as that by which the just lives by the gift of God, namely by faith...."[6] Here, in an experience which Luther describes as being reborn and as entering paradise, a moralistic conscience is redefined in the transmoral.

Again, in Calvin the inevitability of the transmoral conscience is recognized. He maintains that the conscience can never be secure on the basis of achievement. "The sum of the matter then is this,—that if salvation depends on the keeping of the law, the soul can entertain no confidence respecting it, yea, that all promises offered to us by God will become void: we must thus become wretched and lost, if we are sent back to works to find out the cause or the certainty of salvation."[7] He likewise finds our justification not in achievement but in the gracious activity of God engendering faith in our hearts. The following passage from Calvin's *Institutes* sounds much like Luther:

> But Scripture, when it speaks of faith righteousness, leads us to something far different: namely, to turn aside from contemplation of our works and look solely upon God's mercy and Christ's perfection. Indeed, it presents this order of justification: to begin with, God deigns to embrace the sinner with his pure and freely given goodness, *finding nothing in him except his miserable condition* to prompt Him to mercy, since *he sees man utterly void and bare of good works*; and *so he seeks in himself the reason to benefit man.* Then God touches the sinner with a sense of his goodness in order that he, despairing of his own works, may ground the whole of his salvation in God's mercy. This is the experience of faith through which the sinner comes into the possession of his salvation when from the teaching of the gospel he acknowledges that he has been reconciled to God: that with Christ's righteousness interceding and forgiveness of sins accomplished he is justified. And although regenerated by the Spirit of God, he ponders the everlasting righteousness laid up for him not in the good works to which he inclines but in the sole righteousness of Christ.[8]

We note here that our free justification is synonymous with reconciliation to God. In the terminology of our study, the transmoral conscience affirms that our relation to God, the source of our values, is founded upon divine grace rather than on human obedience or achievement.

In a similar vein, Brunner writes, "This is what faith means: to *know* that one is thus 'born again,' to accept life as a gift and righteousness as something outside oneself."[9]

Our theological understanding must be expanded to include this Reformation emphasis upon our justification by faith.

We are ultimately freed from the tyranny of our own ideals only as these are founded in the God who gives Himself to the sinner out of a love which is grounded in His own nature and not in our achievement. In psychological terminology, we are only secure from the tyranny of conscience if that conscience recognizes our right to be (including the security of our relation to the one who is the source of moral authority) prior to any ethical achievements.

It would be wise for us to refer briefly to the traditional dispute between Roman Catholic and Protestant theologians on this issue. The clarification of their differences can serve not only to bridge some unnecessary divisions within Christendom—indeed Hans Küng has argued in *Justification* that Karl Barth's understanding of this matter concurs entirely with Roman Catholic teaching—but also to bring into sharper focus both the theological and the psychological heart of the transmoral conscience.

In essence, the Reformers were seen by Trent as offering a legal fiction (sinners were simply pronounced righteous by God's grace) and thereby as failing to see that God's justifying grace inevitably sanctifies. Witness: "The Catholic doctrine of sanctifying grace ... [states] against the Reformers' conception of justification, that justification truly blots out a man's sins, so that he ceases to be a sinner and becomes just, and that solely by God's deed in the grace of Christ which can never be exacted and never merited." [10] Or again, "Catholic doctrine holds that justification is the event in which God, by a free act of love, brings man into *that relationship with him which a holy God demands* and which the God of overflowing grace is prepared to give him.... This justice, which is not merely imputed in juridical fashion but *makes a man truly just*, is at the same time the forgiveness of sins." [11] It should be noted here that the emphasis remains on God's free grace. Man's moral transformation is a divine work, not a human achievement. But that work is inextricably a work of ethical reformation; it is more than what appeared to be the Reformers' morally permissive divine forgiveness. To use Tillich's terminology, Reformation teaching on justification by faith appeared to Roman Catholics to foster an amoral rather than a transmoral conscience.

97

For their part, the Reformers, influenced no doubt by Luther's reactions against what he believed to be the crude salvation-by-works practice in the Roman Catholic church of his day, struggled to preserve the freedom of divine grace which was for them the only hope for human freedom. Although in their teaching concerning sanctification they gave full recognition to the moral reformation which is an inevitable consequence of grace, they were at pains to preserve the truth as they saw it, that the divine-human relationship was a free and gracious gift from God, brought into being though Christ and experienced as faith, independent of (and therefore expressed usually as prior to) any moral growth in the individual. Thus Luther: "Since then works justify no man but a man must be justified before he can do any good work, it is most evident that it is faith alone which by the mere mercy of God through Christ ... can worthily and sufficiently justify and save the person."[12] Or, taking a more contemporary expression, we find in Brunner, "Before he does anything, he is already in God. In all that he does—without being obliged to search for God—he starts from the fact of his life in God.... He alone can have *peace* with God who no longer strains after God, but who lives in and on God. Peace springs out of a relation with God which is secured by God Himself, that is, the relation of Divine sonship through the gift of God."[13]

Küng has argued that to understand the reality of justification we must look backward to the "divine acquittal of *sinful* man" which he sees as the primary Reformation emphasis in Luther's famous formula, *simul justus et peccator*, at once justified and a sinner, but we must also look forward to the ultimate sanctification of man, promised and thereby already begun. For Küng "the *consummation of justification* has priority over its initial stage. The divine verdict is pre-eminently a pledge and a promise.... The promise refers to the future, but just as the past of man as sinner is man's present, so also his future as justified man is already his present too."[14] One might therefore argue that the clash between the Reformers and Trent was at this point largely a matter of emphasis and terminology. The former, wishing to stress the liberation from the Law granted through grace, the liberation which alone makes it possible for us to stand before God. tended to use the term "justification" with this connotation alone. Trent, desirous of preserving the moral earnestness of the faith, the sanctifying power of God, saw justification more in these terms. Thus to a degree the two sides argued past each other.

This treatment, to be sure, has been sketchy and inevitably oversimplifies some of the intricacies of the theological debate of the time. However, it may serve to illumine the tension within the transmoral conscience in the experience of a totally free right to be, coupled with a deep sense of the call to moral transformation. The Reformers sought to preserve this tension by limiting the connotation of justification to the former moment. (Whether or not this is most in keeping with the original meaning in Saint Paul, it does reflect an important and healing human insight.) Their full treatment of the transmoral conscience, however, requires the recognition of the other pole expressed in their doctrine of sanctification. It was the need to hold the two sides of this tension at once which undoubtedly lay behind the Roman Catholic use of a broader connotation for justification.

The parallels between the Reformers' emphasis upon justification by faith as an experience of the freedom to be before God, prior to any moral achievement, and the therapeutic power of acceptance described in both Freudian and Rogerian therapy will surely strike the reader at once. Indeed Paul Tillich has suggested that "theology had to learn from the psychoanalytic method the meaning of grace, the meaning of forgiveness as acceptance of those who are unacceptable and not of those who are the good people."[15] Freud early in his career abandoned hypnosis and abreaction (a technique more akin to behavior modification than to later psychoanalytic practice) in favor of free association, which he called the fundamental rule of therapy. The patient had to put his self-criticism out of action and tell the therapist all, including those ideas and associations which were disagreeable, indiscreet, unpleasant, or even nonsensical. Therapy functioned insofar as a systematic neutralization of all self-censorship could be awakened. When experienced emotionally, this led to transference, a pseudoloving relationship in which "the patient puts the analyst in the place of his father ... giving him the power which his superego exercises over the ego."[16] In effect, transference recreated the individual's relation to authority, yet the patient's new sense that he was accepted by the therapist gave him the freedom to challenge his conscience and thereby be open to face the full depths of his own being—whatever was revealed. While client-centered therapy speaks of overcoming "conditions of worth" to achieve greater congruence of self and experience, basically the therapeutic process rests upon the same fundamental experience of acceptance, here called "unconditional positive regard," honoring the person "irrespective of the differential values one might place on his specific behaviour."[17] Thus, as the patient

> expresses more and more of the hidden and awful aspects of himself, he finds the therapist showing a consistent and unconditional positive regard for him and his feelings. Slowly he moves toward taking the same attitude toward himself, accepting himself as he is, and therefore ready to move forward in the process of becoming.[18]

> For the client, this optimal therapy would mean an exploration of increasingly strange and unknown and dangerous feelings in himself, the exploration proving possible only because he is gradually realizing that he is accepted unconditionally.[19]

Assuredly, the theological account of acceptance goes beyond the psychotherapeutic in raising the issue of the ultimate source of acceptance. Is the patient's only security the unconditional positive regard of the therapist or the freedom to be himself granted in the womb of the encounter group? How can he then continue to sing the Lord's song of therapeutic wholeness in the Babylonian exile of the real world? The ultimate basis for therapeutic success is a deeper source of acceptance, a more fundamental power to heal. It is the gift of God. But here one enters the realm of faith.

> There is a tacit ontological assumption of all effective therapy not that it is merely the counselor who accepts the client but that the client is acceptable as a human being by the ground of being itself, and that the final reality we confront in life is for us—Deus pro nobis.... The implicit ontological assumption of all effective psychotherapy is made explicit in the Christian proclamation.[20]

One is here reminded of a portion of one of Tillich's famous sermons:

It is as though a voice were saying: "You are accepted. *You are accepted*, accepted by that which is greater than you, and the name of which you do not know. Do not ask for the name now; perhaps you will find it later. Do not try to do anything now; perhaps later you will do much. Do not seek for anything; do not perform anything; do not intend anything. *Simply accept the fact that you are accepted!*" [21]

(The therapist, of course, need not agree with this understanding of the ultimate basis of all acceptance in order to be an instrument of effective psychotherapy.)

Sanctification.—In affirming the necessity of a transmoral conscience, Tillich reminds his readers of the danger when such a conscience ceases to be transmoral and achieves a false liberty by becoming amoral. He is but acknowledging the other moment of grace which was the concern of Roman Catholic theologians in the debate on justification. If such error is to be avoided in our proposed understanding of conscience, a firm relationship must be maintained between the moral and transmoral consciences, that is, between the doctrines of Justification by Faith and the Three Uses of the Law. For Luther and Calvin, as we have said, this relationship is conveyed in their understanding of sanctification.

1. To begin with, the call for sanctification is an acknowledgment that the Christian's spiritual movement does not cease with his reconciliation to God, that the divine love and mercy proclaimed in our free justification by faith in no way abolishes the reality of the demand for righteousness proclaimed by the Law. God loves the sinner but continues to hate the sin.

The two Reformers could describe sanctification alternately as the work of God and as a task assigned to man. In his *Greater Catechism*, Luther connects it with the activity of the Holy Spirit.

But the sanctification, once begun, daily increases; we look for our flesh to perish and be buried with all its corruption, from which it will rise glorified, and in complete and perfect holiness in a new, eternal life. For now we are only in part pure and holy, so that the Holy Spirit is continually at work with us, by means of the Word of God, and daily bestowing forgiveness on us, till we reach that

> life where there is no more forgiveness, all persons there
> being pure and holy. . . . [22]

Depending upon one's interpretation of the phrase "at work with us," Luther may be affirming here the human role in sanctification, but in either case the emphasis is clearly upon sanctification as a divine work. Calvin repeatedly refers to "the gift of regeneration." He declares that "God wipes out in his elect the corruptions of the flesh"[23] and that He "instructs by their reading of [the Law] those whom he inwardly instills with a readiness to obey."[24] Yet obviously sanctification is also an assignment given to man. As outlined in my second chapter, the proclamation of the third use of the law (which is common to our three theologians) is predicated on the assumption of individual responsibility in this matter. Law is seen as a source of exhortation and guidance; it is an instrument in our continuous battle against the "old man." Our duty as Christians, Calvin declares, is to strive to fulfill the law even though this goal will ever exceed our achievements. Likewise Luther, whose theology places great emphasis upon the liberty of faith, leaves no doubt concerning our call to arms in the moral struggle of regeneration.

> For we are not called to a life of ease ... but to labour
> against passions which would not be without guilt (for they
> are truly sins and damnable indeed) unless the mercy of
> God did not impute them. But he does not impute them
> only to those who fight aggressively against their vices,
> invoking the grace of God. Wherefore let him who comes
> to confession not suppose he can lay down his burdens and
> live quietly, but let him know that with the burden laid
> down, God's warfare is on, and he takes on another burden for God against the Devil and his own domestic vices.[25]

The Reformation witness to our justification by faith does not sanction any lessening of the Christian moral imperative. Indeed, Wilhelm Niesel reminds us that Calvin chose to describe the doctrine of regeneration before his doctrine of justification in order to forestall any objections by Roman Catholics that the Protestant emphasis turns faith into a soporific.[26] We bear an individual responsibility with respect to our sanctification. At the same time, though, the Reformers affirm that santification is ultimately the gift of God and thereby forestall any tendency to see it as a religion of works.

  2. I shall merely allude to a second aspect of sanctifica-

tion, since it carries us beyond the specific scope of this study into an analysis of the values comprising the Christian conscience. As indicated earlier, Luther sees the service of the faithful to be motivated by spontaneous love and gratitude toward God, while Calvin lays his emphasis upon working for the glory of God. In either case, the motivation stands in direct contrast to the self-interest so basic to the unbeliever's moral obedience. Sanctification involves a revolution in personal values. The creation of a Christian conscience requires the change in motivation implied in the distinction between the positive and negative conscience. Still, a man may give wholehearted allegiance to lofty ideals but be prompted by selfish reasons. Thus, while we yet affirm that the dynamics of the Christian moral life will be those primarily of the positive conscience, the theological sense has overtones not conveyed by the psychological. Allegiance is not only unambivalent but is truly guided by selfless love, for there is nothing which must be earned. All is a gift.

3. The doctrines of Justification and Sanctification which to this point have been simply juxtaposed are brought into intimate relationship by Luther and Calvin in terms of the experience of faith. The faith which justifies also sanctifies, for it binds us in a deeply personal relationship with Christ wherein we experience His love—knowing thereby that we have been reconciled to God—and respond in love toward him, desiring to become like our Lord.

Faith for Luther is more than cognitive awareness; it is a transforming relationship with Christ. Philip S. Watson summarizes Luther's view:

> It is a fundamental principle for Luther that in faith itself Christ is present ... so that "when we believe that Christ came *for us*, He dwells in our hearts by such faith and purifies us daily by His own proper work." This means that the believer, who is united with Christ "even more closely than the husband is coupled with his wife," must naturally share in Christ's conflict and victory. For the marriage of the believing soul to Him is a matter "not only of communion, but of a blessed strife and victory and salvation and redemption."[27]

A similar understanding underlies Calvin's theology. "Christ was given to us by God's generosity, to be grasped and possessed by us in faith. By partaking of him, we principally receive a double grace: namely, that being reconciled to God through Christ's blamelessness, we may have in heaven instead of a Judge a gracious Father; and secondly, that sanctified by Christ's spirit we may cultivate blamelessness and purity of life."[28] Niesel emphasizes this in his interpretation of Calvin's theology. He remarks, "Calvin has already taught us that mere faith has no significance for salvation but that it acquires saving value only by reference to its object: Jesus Christ. But this Christ whom we receive in faith through the action of the Holy Spirit does not leave us undisturbed in our old manner of life which was hostile to God, but *attracts us* into His own dying and rising again."[29] Justification and sanctification are united in the inclusive, personal relationship with Christ which is faith. There is no justifying faith which does not at the same time involve our regeneration: justification and sanctification presuppose each other in the unity of experience which is faith. "Therefore," Calvin writes, "Christ justifies no one whom he does not at the same time sanctify. These benefits are joined together by an everlasting bond, so that those whom he illumines, he redeems; those whom he redeems, he justifies; those whom he justifies, he sanctifies."[30]

Let me emphasize again that the Reformers' understanding of faith as a personal relationship with Christ does not blur the necessary distinction between justification and sanctification. Both are essential and inevitable in the saving encounter with God in Christ, but justification remains the first of two equals. This relationship is grounded in the free grace of God, redeeming man before and apart from all sanctification. Luther's emphasis upon passive righteousness specifically dissociates justification from all human achievement. Meanwhile Calvin, describing our justification, affirms that God "seeks in himself the reason to benefit man."[31] Niesel quotes Calvin as if to underline this aspect of the Genevan's thought.

> If God were to pronounce us just in consideration of the new life which is in us and will one day fill our souls completely, then we could not avoid asking whether we should ever be able to stand before God. "But God does not graciously accept us because He sees our change for the better, as if conversion were the basis of forgiveness; He comes into our lives, taking us just as we are out of pure mercy."[32]

In the same vein, Gordon Rupp charges Karl Holl with distorting Luther's position in an attempt to play up the Reformer's recognition of the moral imperative. Holl unites justification and sanctification by including the latter in the former. Justification for Luther, he claims, involves not only declaring man righteous but also making him so. It thus becomes an analytic judgment, based upon man's anticipated regeneration. However, Rupp counters, "if justification is a proleptic judgment, then the whole process of justification is set under the sign of Law," which in no way accords with Luther's protest that law must be denied.[33] Here again, then, is the basic difference between the Reformers and Trent.

In summary, therefore, by uniting justification and sanctification in the one experience of faith, the Reformers elevate the Christian conscience into the transmoral sphere. Faith indeed involves man's "participation in a reality which transcends the sphere of moral commands," in a gratuitous relation to divine love. Man is thereby saved from the tyranny of his own ideals. Such liberty is nonetheless achieved without denying the validity of the moral imperative, for bound in the nexus of God's justifying love, man is drawn spontaneously to seek to do His holy will. Throughout this study, conscience has been interpreted via man's diverse relations to his authority figures and their ideals. The Christian conscience, we now see, is the product of a specific, personal relation, the relation to Christ which is faith.

Can we (as with the doctrine of Justification by Faith) discern in this theological account a "psychological" image of the relationship which lies at the heart of a transmoral conscience, a conscience uniting justification and sanctification, acceptance and moral challenge? Is there a parallel between this discussion of sanctification and faith and the practice of counseling, as there was between the Reformers' understanding of Justification by Faith and the power of therapeutic acceptance? In short, can new light be thrown upon the therapeutic relationship from this theological model?

One can hardly expect the therapist as therapist, especially when dealing with non-Christian clients, to preach faith in Christ. But put into simple and less specifically confessional terms, the Reformers' experience of faith suggests that the transmoral conscience arises out of an unambiguous positive attraction toward a moral yet gracious other. If we are not moved by wholehearted love for that moral authority and its standards, then we live under the tyranny of the negative conscience. If that authority is not truly moral, we lapse into a submoral conscience. (It is amoral if it lacks a moral imperative and offers cheap grace—whatever we do is all right: He'll always say, "I forgive"; it is immoral if the qualities expressed therein are unworthy—we can, after all, choose an Adolph Eichmann or an Al Capone for our hero.) If that other is not gracious, then we live under the tyranny of that which we love, the moralism of the positive conscience.

Tillich spoke of a voice which said, *"You are accepted, accepted by that which is greater than you, the name of which you do not know."* Nor do we need to know the name to know acceptance. The unconditional positive regard, the free and unshakable acceptance of the therapist can be an instrument in mediating this power, whether or not the patient, or even the therapist, thinks in these religious terms. To this I now would add that complete fulfillment of our humanness lies in experiencing the magnetic moral power of that "final reality that we confront in life." While this too is part of the Christian proclamation, it is the actual encounter more than the perfection of our theological formulations, the experience of a morally alluring graciousness at the heart of life more than knowledge of the name "Jesus," which ultimately heals. The counselor's task is to be an instrument mediating this encounter which religious men have called a meeting with God, an experience of faith. This is likewise possible whether or not the counselor's own conceptualization of the process moves beyond the therapeutic to religious categories.

Let us be clear as to the flow of the argument. In the discussion of acceptance and justification, we began with the psychology of Freud and Rogers, with the experienced power of therapeutic acceptance, subsequently drawing attention to the similarities between this and the Reformers' description of justification. The theologian could then seek the depth dimension of this experience which would bring him to the ultimate source of acceptance, to the love and forgiveness of God. Therapy works not simply because the counselor accepts us—we cannot linger indefinitely in the cloistered security of the counseling session—

but because there is an empowering acceptance at the heart of life. Whether or not therapist or patient recognizes this fact, this is the reality which is at work. Our treatment of sanctification and faith began with the opposite pole. It started with theology, with the religious imperative to witness to the Law of God, to His call for moral reformation, asserting that the ultimate ground of moral experience is divine. But there again we could note the parallels between the Reformers' call for sanctification and the role of moral confrontation in therapy. Just as acceptance by the therapist points beyond itself to the love of God, so too his ethical interventions can witness to more than his own limited perception of such truth. The urgency of this confrontation arises not simply from the counselor's ethical concerns but from the character of ultimate reality. The moral imperative arises finally not from society but from God. Moreover, we noted that the Reformers experienced a harmonization of justification and sanctification, of acceptance and moral challenge, in the reality they called faith. Here our argument reversed its direction. Having detailed this religious experience of harmony, we then inquired as to the implicit psychodynamics of such an experience, the relation to moral authority underlying such a transmoral conscience. This we found to be the encounter with a morally alluring but equally gracious other, with an authority that attracts our fullest efforts for personal reformation while at the same time granting us the right to be apart from that reformation. There seems to be no grounds to deny the possibility of such a relationship.

Clearly the counselor's own fallibility and weakness do not prevent his fulfillment of this role, any more than his finite capacity to be entirely accepting prevents therapy. He must not, however, confuse allegiance to himself with allegiance to the truly gracious and holy Other at the center of reality, for such would indeed be conducive to the new dependence Freud criticized. In psychological terms, the client must work through his transference; in theological terms, he must come to base his security and moral convictions upon a surer foundation than allegiance to the counselor, whether secular therapist or spiritual director. Equally, the therapist must never forget that he can but witness to the ethical depths of life; he does not possess infallible moral insight. He is not God, however much the patient may tend to deify him in the transference relationship. Nevertheless, he can enrich the experience of therapeutic acceptance through the creative encounter with an ethical witness, the quality of his counsel being influenced by the quality of his own relation to moral values. Where justification and sanctification are meaningfully united in a "faith" experience, where he has found the freedom and moral responsibility of the transmoral conscience, he will be more likely to convey this unity to the other. Knowing that his own right to be is founded not upon achievement but upon free grace, he will recognize that his relation to the client must also grant priority to love over achievement. In this act he will be proclaiming with his whole being that the client's conscience must seek its security in grace, thus inviting the creation of a *nonmoralistic* morality. Yet because the therapist's experience also includes an impetus for moral growth, a sense of the inevitable ethical dimensions of life, this too will find expression in their relationship. Insofar as this is united to his security in grace, he will be able to witness to a nonmoralistic *morality* in his therapeutic office.

Some years ago I was called to a home in crisis. The wife had just returned from an extended trip, visiting friends, and had confessed to her husband that she had had an affair with a man she met in a bar. The husband was hurt, angry, and confused. He could not understand her behavior, especially in view of the great love she professed for their four children. In subsequent conversations, the woman suggested to me that what she must do was return to the other city and find the mysterious lover, to see if it had really all been quite foolish. My opportunity and challenge at that moment, I believed, was to witness carefully to the moral realities of the situation as I saw it. Another affair would but inflame the moral sore and quite probably exacerbate her psychological turmoil as well. Whether or not one agrees fully with my ethical stance is not the issue. It was more important that she be challenged with this dimension of the situation than that my understanding be correct. Only to accept her could have been to suggest that I saw no moral issue in her situation. In addition, it could well be a posture adopted out of fear that an overt ethical witness might cause me to suffer the pain of rejection.

To be sure, in such situations one would not be likely to begin with the flat assertion, "That would be sinful!" The counselor has a responsibility to foster a relationship conducive to hearing an ethical claim. Still, as already suggested, this witness could have taken the form of a moral rebuke. If convinced that she was largely at ease with her actions, that she sensed no moral failure in her conduct, I might have told her that what she had done was wrong. (This would not be to assume that all the responsibility for the situation was hers.) I might have sought to elicit some sense of guilt, some creative moral anxiety which could open the way for a new confrontation with her plight. This approach, while therapeutically and ethically necessary at times, would not, of course, lead us beyond the dangers of moralism; it would not bring us to the fullest form of ethical maturity. At best it could only be the first stage of a longer process.

In this particular case, however, I saw no need for a rebuke. She was already beset by deep feelings of guilt or shame. Yet the path she had chosen out of her dilemma was one I felt to be both morally and therapeutically wrong, and so I said as much. But at the same moment I sought to convey to her that her right to be, specifically her right to be in her relation to me, did not depend upon following my advice. (There may be times when in order to bear full witness to some value, one might say that a relationship will be severed as long as the other continues in certain actions, yet such cannot be the final state of the relationship if the greatest moral growth is to occur.) Here my task was to present a careful and caring moral challenge. The measure of my success, in turn, would depend upon good fortune, my skills as a counselor, and her response to an attempt to proclaim a gracious morality. The fundamental point, however, was that I did not need to sever the moral witness from the healing encounter.

Another instance. Some years before this I trained as a clinical chaplain in a penitentiary. There I had occasion to work for an extended period with a young homosexual. Since his late teens he had been able to make a good living by dressing as a woman and working the night streets as a prostitute. Indeed, so successful was he at female impersonation that he had been an undetected member in the soprano section of a church choir for over a year. His arrest and sentence to our institution was for soliciting. I had no illusions that through counseling I would be able to transform him into a normally functioning heterosexual.

My therapeutic goals were strictly limited. I would be content if I could at least develop some real insight into how he thought and felt. Over a period of some two months, we met regularly for "counseling" and shared many ideas. One day he remarked that he wanted to do something for me. It was clear to him that I did not approve of his life-style, that many of our values were in sharp conflict, but he said, "I appreciate the fact that you have not rejected me as a person. It means a lot to me." Out of gratitude he offered to teach me how to pass for a woman. (I must admit relief when he added that I possessed no natural talent but, provided I was willing to work very hard at it, he thought it could be done.) Clearly there was no therapeutic success here, if success meant "curing" his homosexual tendencies. But to decide in advance that such was the only acceptable measure of progress would be to place myself and also this man under the tyranny of my expectations. We cannot prescribe the time or the nature of the therapeutic impact of such encounters. His experience of acceptance coupled with a clear ethical witness could have opened the way for healing later in his life, even in areas quite unrelated to his homosexuality. We should observe, in any case, that his experience of a moral stance which challenged his whole way of life did not in itself prevent his experiencing a sense of acceptance.

Tensions will remain between psychology and ethics, between mental health and social reform. While holding these two functions together in ourselves, we must still decide at any moment where the emphasis belongs. When do we shift roles to come on forcefully and demandingly with a client who is enjoying a false security in therapy? When do we begin his education to moral reality? Conversely, in the process of moral education, whether in therapy or social action, when do we need to concentrate upon awakening in the other a sense of grace, of his right to be as a free gift, in order that he might gain the freedom to risk a deep, personal transformation? This dilemma will remain, and sincere individuals will disagree on timing and approach.

I have not presented a formula for automatic success. Our client, patient, parishioner, or friend may still respond to any moral confrontation as a personal assault. The reformation in life-style which it seems to suggest may be experienced as too threatening or demanding too great a change. Our attempt at expressing a gracious moral witness may be met only with hostility, flight, or indifference. He may reject our challenge, and we will need the assurance of our right to fail. Yet like law in its initial uses, it may also serve as the first step in challenging the other to confront the full moral realities of his situation. Even then, we may achieve no more than reluctant compliance under the impact of a heightened negative conscience. Yet it could also be preparing the ground for the experience of the transmoral conscience. However imperfectly, we may still be witnessing to the possibility of a nonmoralistic morality, founded upon the encounter with a morally alluring graciousness, with that which theists have called the holy and loving God.

The tensions with which we began have not disappeared, but we can see them now as part of a larger unity. If the full "psychological" model of morality expressed by the Reformers is valid, especially in their description of faith, then such uneasiness need not divide our personalities or our relationships. We can still choose to heal and to challenge.

Some may be disappointed that I have not written a manual, a "how-to" book, although our discussion has not been devoid of practical implications. We will all need to continue the struggle, through success and failure, to improve our skills. But there is no one technique, for counselors naturally have their individual personalities and styles, and therapists trained in widely differing modes can successfully assist others to greater health. My focus has been something which I consider more fundamental: the character and self-understanding of the therapist. If we assume that there is an inevitable clash between acceptance and moral confrontation, we shall be unlikely ever to attempt bringing them into fruitful harmony. If that harmony has not fully come alive in our own person through the "faith" experience, then this dissidence will reduce our therapeutic effectiveness, whatever our technique. It is ultimately the character of the counselor as much as his technique which is crucial.

Notes

Chapter 1

1. Ananias Mpunzi, "Black Theology as Liberation Theology," in *A Reader in Political Theology*, ed. Alister Kee (Philadelphia: Westminster Press, 1974), p. 131.

2. Peter L. Berger, *Invitation to Sociology* (Garden City, N.Y.: Anchor Books, 1963), pp. 158–59.

3. Allen Wheelis, *The Quest for Identity* (New York: W. W. Norton & Co., 1958), p. 165.

4. Reuben Fine, *Freud: A Critical Re-Evaluation of His Theories* (New York: David McKay Co., 1962), p. 73.

5. Albert Ellis, *Sex without Guilt* (New York: Lyle Stuart, 1958), p. 51.

6. Ibid., p. 65.

7. Cf. the anthropological gospel of tolerance; see Frank E. Hartung, "Cultural Relativity and Moral Judgments," *Philosophy of Science* 21 (1954): 118–26.

8. Paul Tillich, "The Theology of Pastoral Care," *Pastoral Psychology* 10 (October 1959): 22.

9. Heinz Hartmann, *Psychoanalysis and Moral Values* (New York: International Universities Press, Inc., 1960), p. 55.

10. Robert A. Harper, *Psychoanalysis and Psychotherapy—36 Systems* (Englewood Cliffs, N.J.: Prentice-Hall, Inc., 1959), p. 86.

11. For a discussion of the theological significance of disease, see Aarne Siirala, *The Voice of Illness* (Philadelphia: Fortress Press, 1964).

12. Daniel D. Williams, *The Minister and the Care of Souls* (New York: Harper & Bros., 1961), p. 13.

13. Wayne Oates, *The Religious Dimensions of Personality* (New York: Association Press, 1957), p. 26.

14. "Fact" is used here in the sense of value-free judgments of the given. Unfortunately, all too often this is assumed to be the totality of truth, and values are denied cognitive status. I have argued elsewhere for the possibility of "moral facts": see John Hoffman, "On Theology's Cognitive Claims: A. J. Ayer Revisited," *Studies in Religion/ Sciences religieuses* 6 (1976): 117–26.

Chapter 2

1. Martin Luther, *A Commentary on St. Paul's Epistle to the Galatians* (Westwood, N.J.: Fleming H. Revell Co., 1953), p. 298.
2. Emil Brunner, *The Divine Imperative* (Philadelphia: Westminster Press, 1947), p. 142.
3. John Calvin, *Institutes of the Christian Religion* (Philadelphia: Westminster Press, 1960), 2.7.6.
4. Luther, *Commentary*, p. 153.
5. Ibid., p. 303.
6. Calvin, *Institutes*, 2.7.10.
7. Luther, *Commentary*, p. 297.
8. Ibid., p. 348.
9. Calvin, *Institutes*, 2.7.12.
10. Ibid.
11. Ibid., 3.6.3.
12. Ibid., 2.7.12.
13. John Calvin, *Instruction in Faith* (Philadelphia: Westminster Press, 1949), pp. 41–42.
14. Luther, *Commentary*, p. 302 (emphasis mine).
15. Martin Luther, "Concerning Christian Liberty," in *Luther's Primary Works*, ed. Henry Wace and C. A. Buchheim (London: Hodder & Stoughton, 1896), p. 262.
16. Luther, *Commentary*, p. 52.
17. Contextual or situation ethics is an approach to moral decision making which rejects the idea that one should reach such conclusions basically by the application of a code or law, appealing instead to a general and sometimes rather vague notion of love. Witness Joseph Fletcher: "The situationist enters every decision-making situation fully armed with the ethical maxims of his community and its heritage, and he treats them with respect as illuminators of his problem. Just the same, he is prepared in any situation to compromise them or set them aside *in the situation* if love seems better served by doing so" (*Situation Ethics* [Philadelphia: Westminster Press, 1966], p. 26).
18. G. Wingren, *Luther on Vocation* (Philadelphia: Muhlenberg Press, 1957), p. 199.
19. We shall return to the discussion of justification by faith in chap. 5.

20. Martin Luther, "Preface to the Epistle of Paul to the Romans," in *Selected Works of Martin Luther*, ed. Henry Cole (London: W. Simpkin & R. Marshall, 1826), 1:205.
21. Ibid., pp. 208–9.
22. For a discussion of law and situation ethics, see John Hoffman, "Contextual Ethics and Personal Identity," *Studies in Religion/Sciences religieuses* 1 (1971): 116–27.
23. Martin Luther, "A Treatise concerning Good Works," in *Selected Works of Martin Luther*, 2:444.
24. Ibid., p. 492.
25. Martin Luther, *Sermons on the Most Interesting Doctrines of the Gospel* (London: James Duncan, 1830), p. 218.
26. Calvin, *Institutes*, 3.19.4.
27. Luther, "Preface," p. 205.
28. Brunner, p. 150.
29. Ibid., p. 149.
30. To follow his discussion it is essential to remember the central place which he gives to the divine command in the life of faith. Consequently, the law is always understood as an instrument of that command in the context of decision.
31. Brunner, p. 179.
32. Ibid., p. 233.

Chapter 3

1. D. O. Hebb, *A Textbook of Psychology* (Philadelphia: W. B. Saunders Co., 1958), p. 259.
2. C. S. Hall and G. Lindzey, *Theories of Personality* (New York: John Wiley & Sons, 1957), p. 13.
3. Readers who would gain a fuller understanding of this approach could refer to such works as *Behavior Modification*, ed. W. Stewart Agras (Boston: Little, Brown & Co., 1972); or A. Robert Sherman, *Behavior Modification: Theory and Practice* (Monterey, Calif.: Brooks/Cole Publishing Co., 1973).
4. B. F. Skinner, *Science and Human Behavior* (New York: Free Press, 1965), pp. 34–35.
5. Interestingly enough, the psychologist who proposed the "bell and pad" treatment for enuresis was O. Hobart Mowrer, cited in chap. 1 above as supporting the necessity for moral values in counseling (O. H. Mowrer, "Appara-

tus for the Study and Treatment of Enuresis," *American Journal of Psychology* 51 [1938]: 163).

6. Sigmund Freud, "The Defence Neuro-Psychoses," in *Collected Papers* (London: Hogarth Press, 1953), 1:61.

7. Sigmund Freud, "The Aetiology of Hysteria," ibid., p. 185.

8. Ibid., p. 193.

9. Sigmund Freud, "Further Remarks on the Defence Neuro-Psychoses," ibid., p. 162.

10. Fine, p. 77.

11. Sigmund Freud, *Civilization and Its Discontents* (New York: Jonathan Cape & Harrison Smith, 1949), p. 120.

12. Ibid., p. 121 (emphasis mine).

13. In *The Ego and the Id* (London: Hogarth Press, 1949), as in numerous other passages, Freud points to the reality of a need for punishment. He remarks that "in many criminals, especially youthful ones, it is possible to detect a very powerful sense of guilt which existed before the crime, and is not therefore the result of it but its motive" (p. 76). This phenomenon, I think, becomes comprehensible in the light of ambivalence. The individual accepts the very rules which he has rejected and violated, even if the violation in fact is only an unconscious wish. Consequently it becomes understandable that punishment is also accepted as right and is actually sought after.

14. Carl R. Rogers, *On Becoming a Person* (Boston: Houghton Mifflin Co., 1961), p. 32.

15. Ibid., p. 62.

16. Carl R. Rogers, *Client-centered Therapy* (Boston: Houghton Mifflin Co., 1951), p. 45.

17. Ibid., p. 223.

18. Ibid., p. 224.

19. Rogers, *On Becoming a Person*, pp. 384–402.

20. Rogers, *Client-centered Therapy*, p. 48.

21. Carl R. Rogers, "A Theory of Therapy, Personality, and Interpersonal Relationships as Developed in the Client-centered Framework," in *Psychology: A Study of a Science*, ed. Sigmund Koch (New York: McGraw-Hill Book Co., 1959), 3:209.

22. Rogers, *On Becoming a Person*, pp. 168–70.

23. Rogers, "A Theory of Therapy," pp. 234–35.

24. Rogers, *Client-centered Therapy*, p. 30.

25. Rogers, *On Becoming a Person*, p. 187.
26. Ibid., p. 177.
27. Rogers, "A Theory of Therapy," p. 206.
28. Rogers, *Client-centered Therapy*, p. 48.
29. Freud, *The Ego and the Id*, p. 72.
30. Sigmund Freud, *A General Introduction to Psychoanalysis* (New York: Garden City Publishing Co., 1943), p. 377.
31. Philip Rieff, *Freud: The Mind of the Moralist* (New York: Viking Press, 1959), pp. 321–22.
32. Rogers, *Client-centered Therapy*, p. 20.
33. Rogers, "A Theory of Therapy," p. 221.
34. A. Maslow, *Motivation and Personality*, quoted in Rogers, *On Becoming a Person*, p. 174.
35. Rogers, *Client-centered Therapy*, p. 169.
36. Rogers, *On Becoming a Person*, p. 194.
37. Ibid., p. 171.
38. Rogers, *Client-centered Therapy*, p. 150 (emphasis mine).
39. Rogers, "A Theory of Therapy," p. 210.
40. Ibid., p. 225.
41. Sigmund Freud, " 'Civilized' Sexual Morality and Modern Nervousness," in *Collected Papers* (London: Hogarth Press, 1953), 2:86.
42. Sigmund Freud, *The Future of an Illusion* (New York: Liveright Publishing Corp., 1935), p. 12.
43. Sigmund Freud, *Moses and Monotheism* (London: Hogarth Press, 1939), p. 212.
44. Ibid., p. 182.
45. Freud, *Civilization and Its Discontents*, p. 101.
46. Ibid., pp. 133–34.
47. Rogers, *On Becoming a Person*, pp. 177–78.
48. Will Herberg, "Freud, the Revisionists, and Social Reality," in *Freud and the Twentieth Century*, ed. Benjamin Nelson (New York: Meridian Books, 1957), pp. 157–58.
49. Allen Wheelis, *The Moralist* (New York: Basic Books, 1973), p. 11.
50. Reinhold Niebuhr, *The Nature and Destiny of Man* (New York: Charles Scribner's Sons, 1941), 1:236.

Chapter 4
1. Franz Alexander, *The Psychoanalysis of the Total Personality* (New York: Nervous and Mental Disease Publishing Co., 1930), p. xv.

2. Sigmund Freud, "On Narcissism: An Introduction," in *Collected Papers* (London: Hogarth Press, 1953), 4:51.

3. Ibid.

4. Sigmund Freud, *Group Psychology and the Analysis of the Ego* (London: International Psychoanalytic Press, 1922), p. 60.

5. Ibid., p. 61.

6. Ibid.

7. Sigmund Freud, "Some Psychical Consequences of the Anatomical Distinction between the Sexes," in *The Standard Edition of the Complete Psychological Works of Sigmund Freud*, ed. James Strachey et al. (London: Hogarth Press, 1955), 19:250 (emphasis mine).

8. Sigmund Freud, "Libidinal Types," in *Collected Papers* (London: Hogarth Press, 1953), 5:249.

9. Ibid., p. 250.

10. Sigmund Freud, *New Introductory Lectures on Psychoanalysis* (New York: W. W. Norton & Co., 1933), p. 127 (emphasis mine).

11. Rogers, *Client-centered Therapy*, p. 157.

12. Rogers, *On Becoming a Person*, pp. 170–71.

13. Rogers, "A Theory of Therapy," pp. 209–10.

14. Franz Alexander, "Remarks about the Relation of Inferiority Feelings and Guilt Feelings," *International Journal of Psychoanalysis* 19 (1938): 44.

15. Ibid., p. 43.

16. Erik Erikson, *Childhood and Society* (New York: W. W. Norton & Co., 1950), p. 80.

17. Paul W. Pruyser, "Nathan and David: A Psychological Footnote," *Pastoral Psychology* 13 (1962): 18.

18. Gerhart Piers and Milton B. Singer, *Shame and Guilt* (Springfield, Ill.: C. C. Thomas, 1953).

19. Alexander, *The Psychoanalysis of the Total Personality*, p. 19.

20. Ibid.

21. Franz Alexander, *Fundamentals of Psychoanalysis* (New York: W. W. Norton & Co., 1948), p. 84.

22. Heinz Hartmann, *Ego Psychology and the Problem of Adaptation* (New York: International Universities Press, Inc., 1961), p. 94.

23. Odier makes repeated references in his work to Henri Bergson's *The Two Sources of Morality and Religion*.

24. Charles Odier, *Les deux sources consciente et inconsciente de la vie morale* (Neuchâtel: Editions de la Baconnière, 1947), p. 122 (translation mine).

Chapter 5

1. Gotthard Booth, "Problems of Authority for Individual Christians: Its Use and Abuse," *Journal of Pastoral Care* 8 (1954): 203–17.
2. René Spitz, "Hospitalism," *Psychoanalytic Study of the Child* 1 (1945): 53–74; and "Anaclitic Depression," ibid. 2 (1946): 313–42; Lauretta Bender, "Psychopathic Behavior Disorders in Children," in *Handbook of Correctional Psychology*, ed. R. M. Linder and R. V. Seliger (New York: Philosophical Library, 1947), pp. 360–77; and "There Is No Substitute for Family Life," *Child Study* (Spring 1946), p. 96.
3. C. Ellis Nelson, "The Christian Education of Conscience," *Princeton Seminary Bulletin* (September 1961), pp. 37–47.
4. E. Frederick Proelss, "The Ministry of a Prison Chaplain," ibid., pp. 25–36.
5. Piers and Singer, p. 33.

Chapter 6

1. Niebuhr, 1:183–84.
2. Paul Tillich, *The Protestant Era* (Chicago: University of Chicago Press, 1948), p. 145.
3. Ibid., p. 149.
4. Luther, *Commentary*, p. 23.
5. Ibid., p. 351.
6. Quoted in Gordon Rupp, *The Righteousness of God* (London: Hodder & Stoughton, 1953), p. 122.
7. John Calvin, *Commentary on the Epistle of Paul the Apostle to the Romans* (Grand Rapids, Mich.: W. B. Eerdmans, 1947), p. 171.
8. Calvin, *Institutes*, 3.11.16.
9. Brunner, p. 77.
10. Karl Rahner and Herbert Vorgrimler, *Theological Dictionary* (New York: Herder & Herder, 1968), p. 421.
11. Ibid., p. 247 (emphasis mine).
12. Luther, *Christian Liberty*, pp. 275–76.
13. Brunner, p. 78.

14.	Hans Küng, *Justification* (New York: Thomas Nelson & Sons, 1964), pp. 64–65.

15.	Paul Tillich, *Theology of Culture* (New York: Oxford University Press, 1959), p. 124.

16.	Sigmund Freud, *An Outline of Psychoanalysis* (New York: W. W. Norton & Co., 1949), p. 67.

17.	Rogers, "A Theory of Therapy," p. 208.

18.	Rogers, *On Becoming a Person*, p. 63.

19.	Ibid., p. 185.

20.	Thomas C. Oden, *Kerygma and Counseling* (Philadelphia: Westminster Press, 1966), pp. 21, 24.

21.	Paul Tillich, *The Shaking of the Foundations* (New York: Charles Scribner's Sons, 1948), p. 162.

22.	Martin Luther, "The Greater Catechism," in *Luther's Primary Works*, p. 105.

23.	Calvin, *Institutes*, 3.3.9.

24.	Ibid., 2.7.12.

25.	Quoted in Rupp, pp. 181–82.

26.	Wilhelm Niesel, *The Theology of Calvin* (London: Lutterworth Press, 1956), pp. 130–31.

27.	Philip S. Watson, *Let God Be God!* (London: Epworth Press, 1948), p. 167.

28.	Calvin, *Institutes*, 3.2.1.

29.	Niesel, p. 318 (emphasis mine).

30.	Calvin, *Institutes*, 3.16.1.

31.	Ibid., 3.11.16.

32.	Niesel, p. 138.

33.	Rupp, p. 183.

Index

Depth psychology, 31
Desegregation, school, 16
Deux sources consciente et inconsciente de la vie morale, les, 74
Divine Imperative, The, 27

Ego and the Id, The, 39, 58, 73
Ego ideal, 39, 56–60; as conscious conscience in Alexander, 73; genesis of Freudian, 43; as object of love, 57–58; in Odier, 77; and third use of the law, 60. *See also* Positive conscience; Shame
Ego Psychology and the Problem of Adaptation, 75
Ellis, Albert, 7–8
Erikson, Erik, 31, 65–66
Ethics: contextual, 23, 25, 27, 82–83; sexual, 7–8; tension between, and psychology, 1, 49–50, 110–11
Eysenck, H. J., 32

Fact contrasted with values, 15–16
Faith experience, 103–6
Fear, contrast between, and guilt, 78–79
First use of the law, 55, 60, 84–85; behavior modification and, 35; as restraint, 19, 21. *See also* Law
Free-expression child training, 86
Freud, Sigmund, 1, 7, 15, 17, 24, 31–32; contrast between, and Rogers, 44, 50–54; pessimism of, 51–53; similarities between, and Rogers, 44, 46–47; Works: *Civilization and Its Discontents*, 40; *The Ego and the Id*, 39, 58, 73; *The Future of an Illusion*, 52; *Group Psychology and the Analysis of the Ego*, 57; "Libidinal Types," 59; *New Introductory Lectures on Psychoanalysis*, 58–59; "On Narcissism: An Introduction," 57;

Totem and Taboo, 39, 41. *See also* Freudian theory
Freudian theory: acceptance in, and justification by faith, 99–100; ambivalence in, 39; anal personality, 81; conscience equated with superego in, 55, 59; defense neuroses in, 37–38; dependence criticized in, 107; eros versus death in, 52–53; ethic of honesty in, 87; ethical confrontation avoided in, 47–50; fundamental rule in, 99; instinctual conflict in, 52–53; libidinal personality types in, 59; libido theory in, 38; mental illness in, 39; morality as moralistic in, 39, 44, 55; myth of the Fall in, 41; narcissism in, 57; naturalism in, 52; patricide in, 41–42; pre-Oedipal relationships in, 58; successful repression in, 59–60; theological anthropology of, 53; transference in, 99; unconscious morality in, 39, 72. *See also* Ego ideal; Freud; Superego
Future of an Illusion, The, 52

Genocide, 3, 49
Golding, William, 51
Greater Catechism, The, 25, 101
Group Psychology and the Analysis of the Ego, 57
Guilt: ambivalence and, 21, 29; confusion of, with aspiration, 86–88; fear and, 21, 29, 42–43, 78–79; inhibition and, 66–67; shame contrasted with, 65–67; social anxiety and, 40

Häring, Bernard, 18
Hartmann, Heinz, 11, 75–76
Health, 11–12
Hebb, Donald, 31
Herberg, Will, 53

Hobbes, Thomas, 51
Holl, Karl, 105
Honesty, importance of, in counseling, 88, 93
Humanistic psychology, 31, 44

Illness as divine punishment, 61-62
Inferiority feelings. *See* Shame
Institutes, 96
Instruction in Faith, 23

Jung, Carl, 31
Justification, 97
Justification by faith: Brunner on, 96, 98; Calvin on, 95-96; as a gift of God, 95, 97; Hans Küng on, 98; Luther on, 95, 98; and the power of acceptance, 99-101; priority of, over sanctification, 104-5; tension of, with sanctification, 97-99; united with sanctification in faith experience, 103-4

Kierkegaard, Søren, 17
Küng, Hans, 97-98

Law: Christ as content of, 23, 26; civic function of, 19; as civic virtues, 27; as commandment in Luther, 24-25; and contextual ethics, 23, 25, 27; as Divine Command in Brunner, 27; motivation for obedience to, 21, 26-29, 103; as pattern for Christian identity, 23, 26; range of meaning of, 19, 22, 28; of Talion, 61-62; tension of, with gospel, 1; three uses of, 18, 101; *usus paedagogicus*, 20; *usus politicus*, 19; value of negative obedience to, 19, 30. *See also* First use of the law; Second use of the law; Third use of the law
Liberation movements, 3
"Libidinal Types," 59

Lord of the Flies, 51
Love as the foundation of the "psychologically" moral, 42-43, 78-79
Luther: faith experience in, 103; first use of the law in, 19, 21; guilt and fear in, 21, 29; justification by faith in, 95, 104-5; law as commandment in, 24-25; motivation for good works in, 25; primary function of the law in, 23; sanctification in, 101-2; second use of the law in, 20-21; the term "law" in, 24-25; third use of the law in, 23-26; Works: *A Treatise concerning Good Works*, 25; *The Greater Catechism*, 25, 101

Manhattan Project, 16
Marx, Karl, 1
Maslow, Abraham, 31, 48
Menninger, Karl, 8
Moral authorities, disillusionment with, 5-6
Moral automatisms. *See* automatisms, moral
Moralism: and behavior modification, 35-37; concept of, 9, 35; counselor's freedom from the tyranny of, 88, 91; interpersonal generation of, 36; intrapersonal generation of, 41; as manifestation of sin, 91; problem of, in psychotherapy, 8-9, 78; as self-imposed tyranny, 90-91, 93; and the transmoral conscience, 93-111
Moralistic obedience as salutary, 36-37
Morality: as curbing libido in Freudian theory, 38; as inevitable in life and counseling, 3, 9; as moralistic in Freudian theory, 44; nature of, 9, 54; nonmoralistic, 9-10, 93, 106-8;

pseudo, 73-74, 81; psychology
as covert, 6-8, 48-50. *See also*
Law; Unconscious morality
Moral maladaptation, 81-82
Moral rebuke in counseling, 83-86
Moral witness in counseling, 79-
89
Mowrer, O. Hobart, 9
Murder of the father. *See* Freudian
theory, patricide in

Negative conscience, 30, 56-57,
87; in hospital patients, 61-63;
as inevitably moralistic, 90; as a
moral rebuke, 84; as salutary,
85-86. *See also* Superego
Nelson, C. Ellis, 83
*New Introductory Lectures on
Psychoanalysis*, 58-59
Niebuhr, Reinhold, 53, 91
Niesel, Wilhelm, 102, 104
Nondirective counseling. *See*
Rogerian theory

Oates, Wayne, 12
Odier, Charles, 74, 76-77
"On Narcissism: An Introduc-
tion," 57

Passive righteousness, 24-25, 95
Pastoral care, 10-15
Piers, Gerhart, 66, 86
Positive conscience, 30, 56-61, 87;
in hospital patients, 64-65;
possibility of nonmoralistic
morality with, 90; tyranny of,
64-65, 67, 72. *See also* Ego ideal
Prejudice, 82
Proelss, E. Frederick, 84
Pruyser, Paul, 66
*Psychoanalysis of the Total Per-
sonality, The*, 73
Psychology: as covert morality, 6-
8, 48-50; as source for theology,
16-17, 93-94; tension between,
and ethics, 1, 49-50, 110-11

Psychotherapy, 10-15; morality
and, 3-4, 79-89
Punishment as therapeutic, 33

Quest for Identity, The, 6, 8

Reich, Wilhelm, 11
"Remarks about the Relation of
Inferiority Feelings and Guilt
Feelings," 65
Reward and punishment in behavior modification, 32-33
Rieff, Philip, 48, 87
Rogerian theory: acceptance in,
and justification by faith, 100;
client treated as responsible in,
45, 50-51; conditions of worth,
46, 51, 55, 61, 100; congruence
in, 47, 61, 73; ethical confrontation avoided in, 47-50; the Fall
in, 51; mental illness in, 44;
morality as moralistic in, 55;
naturalism in, 53; nondirective
counseling in, 44-45; positive
conscience in, 60-61; theological anthropology of, 53; therapy
emphasized in, 44; unconditional positive regard in, 100
Rogers, Carl R., 15, 17, 24, 31-
32; contrast between, and
Freud, 44, 50-54; covert moral
claims in, 48-50; optimism of,
47-48, 50-51; rejection of
Skinner by, 45; similarities between, and Freud, 44, 46-47.
See also Rogerian theory
Roman Catholic church, 5
Rousseau, Jean-Jacques, 51
Rupp, Gordon, 105

Salinger, J. D., 51
Salvation, 12
Sanctification, 101-8; as divine
work, 102; as human task, 102;
motivation for obedience following, 103; tension of, with justifi-

3 1543 50079 1712

253.5
H699e

DATE DUE

AP 30 '95			
AP 17 '97			

Cressman Library

Cedar Crest College

Allentown, Pa. 18104

DEMCO